MACCLESFIELD - WI

BOLLINGTON · CONGLETON · POYNTON

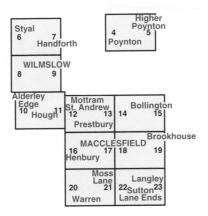

Styal
6   7
Handforth

Higher Poynton
4   5
Poynton

WILMSLOW
8   9

Alderley Edge
10   11
Hough

Mottram St. Andrew
12   13
Prestbury

Bollington
14   15

MACCLESFIELD
16   17 18   19
Henbury

Brookhouse

Moss Lane
20   21
Warren

Langley
22 Sutton 23
Lane Ends

West Heath
26
Congleton

24

25

Every effort has been made to verify the accuracy of information in this book but the publishers cannot accept responsibility for expense or loss caused by an error or omission. Information that will be of assistance to the user of the maps will be welcomed.

The representation on these maps of a road, track or path is no evidence of the existence of a right of way.

Car Park	P
Public Convenience	C
Place of Worship	+
One-way Street	→
Pedestrianized	▨
Post Office	●

Scale of street plans 4 inches to 1 mile
Unless otherwise stated

Street plans prepared and published by ESTATE PUBLICATIONS, Bridewell House, TENTERDEN, KENT, and based upon the ORDNANCE SURVEY mapping with the permission of The Controller of H. M. Stationery Office.

The Publishers acknowledge the co-operation of the local authorities of towns represented in this atlas.

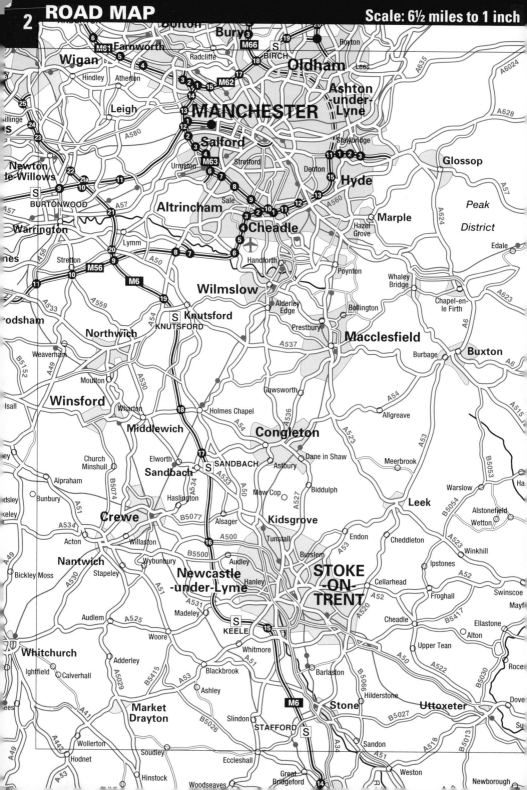

Scale: 7 inches to 1 mile

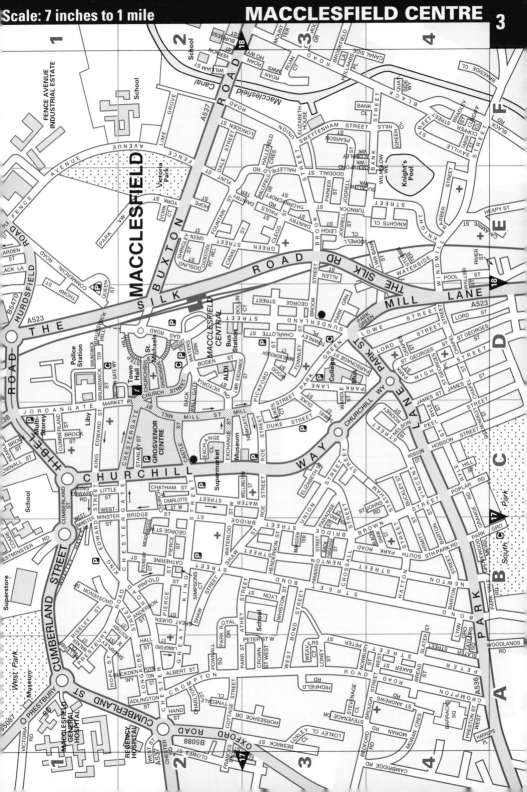

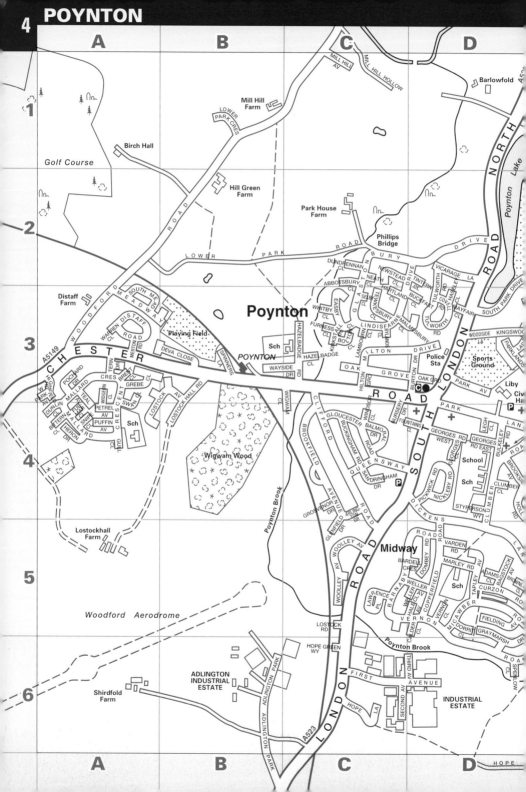

E   F   G   H

Serpentine Wood

MIDDLEWOOD — **1**

New House Farm

Middlewood

MELROSE CRES

DERBYSHIRE RD

Poynton Park

POOL HOUSE RD   HILTON RD — **2**

TOWERS CL

MILSTONE CL

TOWER GDNS

Prince's Wood

PARK DRIVE

TOWERS ROAD DRIVE

Towers Yard Farm

Rabbit Burro Farm

MIDDLEWOOD ROAD

PRINCE

HILTON RD

HAWTHORN GRO

CARLETON RD

PRINCES INCLINE

INCLINE

RINCES

GREEN

ST ELMO PARK

Davenport Golf Club

ROAD GREEN

3

CHARLECOTE RD

HOLKER

ST ELMO

Club House

Davenport Golf Club

LANE GREEN

SULGRAVE AV

MORETON

CHARLECOTE

HARDWICKE RD

BLENHEIM

Marina

DALE HOUSE FOLD

Woodlands Nursing Home

MIDDLEWOOD LANE

ANSON

LANE NORTH

ROAD

4

LYME ROAD

Picnic Site

Fire Sta

WAY

OAKFIELD CRESCENT

SCHOOL

Playing Field

WOBURN

Newtown

Higher Poynton

LONG ROW

Holmelyme House

HOCKLEY

CHESTNUT DRIVE

COPPICE

HEPLEY

TRAFALGAR

Picnic Site

MAPLE AV

ASH

HAZEL DR

CHERRY TREE AV

ELM AV

CHESTNUT DRIVE

PINE

NELSON CL

EATON CL

ROAD COPPICE

SHRIGLEY ROAD NORTH

Macclesfield Canal

5

BIRCH RD

RAINOW

BOSDEN

School

KETTLESHULME WAY

SUTTON

ELM BEDS ROAD

SHELDON RD

School & Leisure Centre

ADLINGTON CL

WARFORD

GAWSWORTH RD

Hockley

SHRIGLEY ROAD SOUTH

Picnic Site

SIDDINGTON

ALDERLEY

WATERLOO LANE

DICKENS ROAD

Wardsend Bridge

NARROW LANE

Poynton Brook

Poynton Coppice

6

Works

LANE

Yewtree Farm

YEW TREE RD

WOOD LA NORTH

Wardsend

LANE

E   F   G   H

A **B** **C** **D**

MANCHESTER
INTERNATIONAL
AIRPORT

BOLSHA RD

Oak Tree Farm

B5166

STYAL ROAD

HOLLIN LANE

WILKINS LANE

LANE

Yew Tree Farm

Club House

MOSS LANE

Styal Golf Course

HOLLIN LANE

HOLLY ROAD

ALTRINCHAM ROAD

Lode Hill Farm

Parkfield

Styal Cross

ALTRINCHAM

Styal

Football Grnd

Cricket Grnd

CLAY LA

ROAD

STANNELANDS

Norcliffe Hall
Nursing Home

Primary School

OAK COTS

P

Chapel

STYAL

STYAL STATION

ROAD

APPRENTICE LA

HOLTS LANE

Cross Farm

SHAWS FOLD

Styal Country Park

Wilmslow Lacrosse Field

Linney's Bridge

ROAD

QUARRY BANK ROAD

P

Bank House Farm

Quarry Bank Mill N.T.

Reservoir

STYAL ROAD

WORMS HILL ROAD

CHURCH AV
CHURCH VW

SYCAMORE CL

Transmitting Station

H.M. Prison

River Bollin

Sewage Works

HOLLY RD

CARR MILL RD

ASHLEY RD

REEMAN

TWINNIES

PAR

Rec Grnd

School

BARLOW

A538

ALTRINCHAM

Stamford Lodge

Rec Grnd

Rugby Ground

STYAL ROAD

P

STAMFORD RD

BOOTH

NEWTON

CRANFORD RD

TRAFFORD

PRESCOTT

CRE

EDERTON RD

OAKMEAN

PLEASAN

CARMEAN

MOBBERLEY RD

ROAD

A538

MOSS LA

NAYS

SUCKLEY

WOODLANDS RD

VAT RD

KINGS RD

CARRWOOD

CRANFORD RD

B5166 STYAL ROAD

GRANGE PAR

A **B** **8** **C** **D**

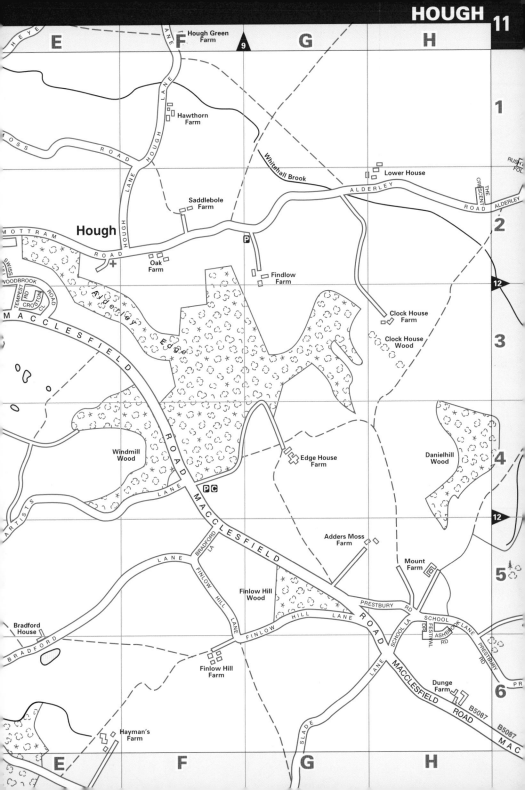

E F G H

HEYE

Hough Green Farm

LANE

HOUGH

9

Hawthorn Farm

MOSS

ROAD

Whitehall Brook

Lower House

ALDERLEY

ROAD

ALDERLEY

RUSH FOL

THE CRESCENT

Saddlebole Farm

LANE

HOUGH

Hough

MOTTRAM

ROAD

P

Oak Farm

Findlow Farm

Clock House Farm

SWISS

WOODBROOK

TEMPEST RD

CROSTON CL

ROAD

Alderley

Edge

Clock House Wood

MACCLESFIELD

ROAD

Windmill Wood

LANE

Edge House Farm

Danielhill Wood

P C

ARTISTS

MACCLESFIELD

Adders Moss Farm

Mount Farm

BRADFORD

LA

LANE

FINLOW HILL LANE

Finlow Hill Wood

FINLOW

HILL

LANE

PRESTBURY RD

ROAD

SCHOOL LA

SCHOOL

FESTIVAL

ASHBROOK RD

DRI

RD

PRESTBURY

RD

Bradford House

BRADFORD

Finlow Hill Farm

LANE

MACCLESFIELD

ROAD

Dunge Farm

B5087

PR

Hayman's Farm

SLADE

B5087

MAC

E F G H

1

2

12

3

4

12

5

6

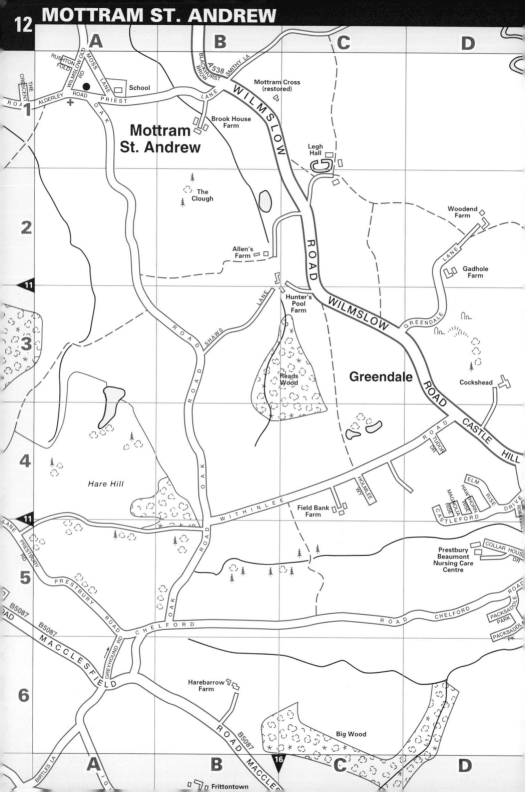

Mottram St. Andrew

Greendale

Hare Hill

Reads Wood

The Clough

School

Brook House Farm

Mottram Cross (restored)

Legh Hall

Woodend Farm

Gadhole Farm

Allen's Farm

Hunter's Pool Farm

Cockshead

Field Bank Farm

Prestbury Beaumont Nursing Care Centre

Collar House

Harebarrow Farm

Big Wood

Frittontown

Macclesfield Road

Wilmslow Road

Chelford Road

Castle Hill

Prestbury Road

Packsaddle Park

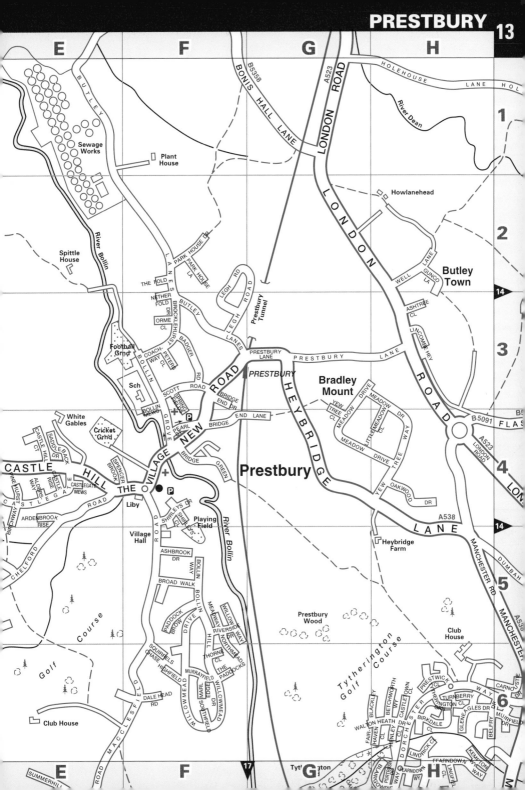

Bollington

Rainow

Grid labels: E F G H across top and bottom; numbers 1, 2, 3, 4, 5, 6 down right side.

Harrop Brook

HEDGEROW HEDGEROW

Winterside Farm

Billinge Hill

SPULEY LANE

ROAD

LONG LANE

LONG GREEN LANE

BEESTON LANE

NAB LA

NAB CT

BERISTOW RISE

COCKSHEADHEY RD

BEESTON MNT

OAK BANK DR

MNT PLEASANT

SHAW LANE

WILLOW BANK

RAINOW RD

INGERSLEY

PALMERSTON ST

CHURCH STREET

CHAPEL LANE

HARROP RD

TURNER ST

TURNER RISE

LOWTHER ST

NANCY

QUEEN

CT

COTTS

KT F

OLDHAM

HIGH

PARK ST

ALLEN ST

CUMBERLAND DR

ADSHEAD

CHANCERY

COW LA

Works

Works

SMITHY BROW

INGERSLEY ROAD

MILL LANE

OAKENBANK

BLAZE

HILL

BLAZE HILL

JUMPER LANE

LANE

OAKENBANK LANE

Savio House

Ingersley Hall Farm

Rainowlow

White Nancy (Monument)

Saddle of Kerridge

Waulkmill Farm

HEDWAY LA

WINDMILL LANE

HIGHER LANE

Bridge Quarry

Kerridge Hill

Sewage Works

Hough-Hole Farm

SUGAR LANE

Back-of-the-Crofts

Clarke House

JUMPER LANE

LANE

Reservoir

B5470

Swanscoe Farm

Rainow

Rainow C.P. School

LINCOLN CL

FOREST CL

JOHNS CL

HOUGH CL

MILLERS MDW

MEADOW

FRITH

CHAPEL

ROBINS CL

MILLERS CT

STOCKS LANE

MOUNT

ROUND MDW

PEDLEY HILL

CHURCH LA

LOWER HILL

LIDGATE LANE

ROAD

Thornset Farm

19

Res

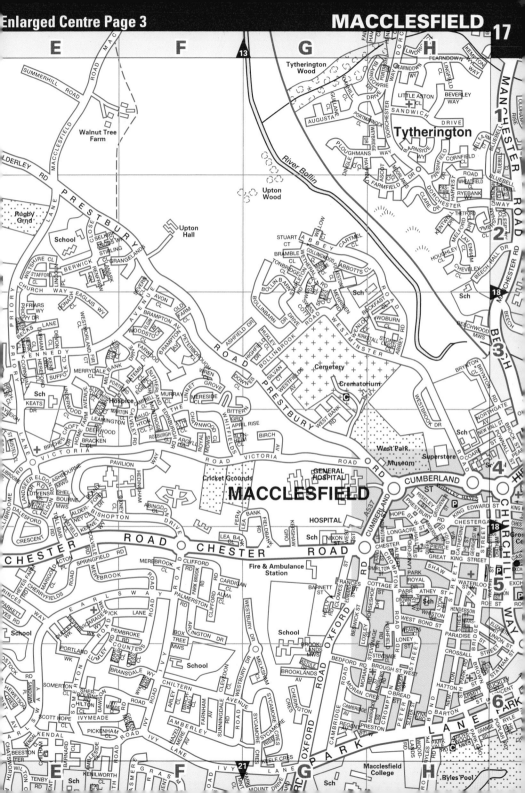

MACCLESFIELD

Tytherington

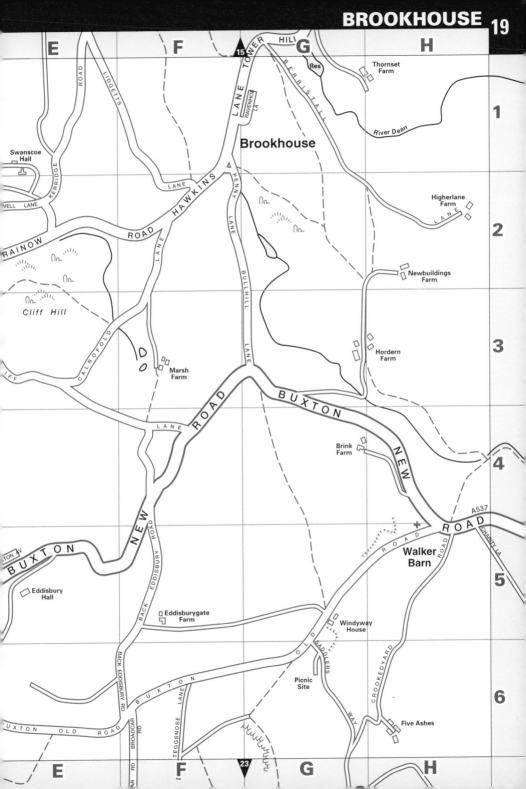

E **F** **G** **H**

1

2

3

4

5

6

TOWER HILL

Thornset Farm

Res

River Dean

RAVENHO LA

Brookhouse

Higherlane Farm

Swanscoe Hall

LIDGETTS ROAD

KERRIDGE ROAD

WELL LANE

LANE

HAWKINS LANE

ROAD

RAINOW

Cliff Hill

CALROFOLD LANE

PENNY LANE

BULLHILL LANE

Marsh Farm

Newbuildings Farm

Hordern Farm

LANE

ROAD

BUXTON

NEW

ROAD

Brink Farm

NEW

Walker Barn

A537

CHARITY LA

BUXTON AV

BUXTON

NEW

BACK EDDISBURY ROAD

Eddisbury Hall

Eddisburygate Farm

ROAD

ROAD

ROAD

Windyway House

OLD SADDLERS

Picnic Site

CROOKEDYARD

WAY

Five Ashes

BACK EDDISBURY RD

BROADCAR RD

TEGGSNOSE LANE

BUXTON LANE

BUXTON OLD ROAD

E **F** **G** **H**

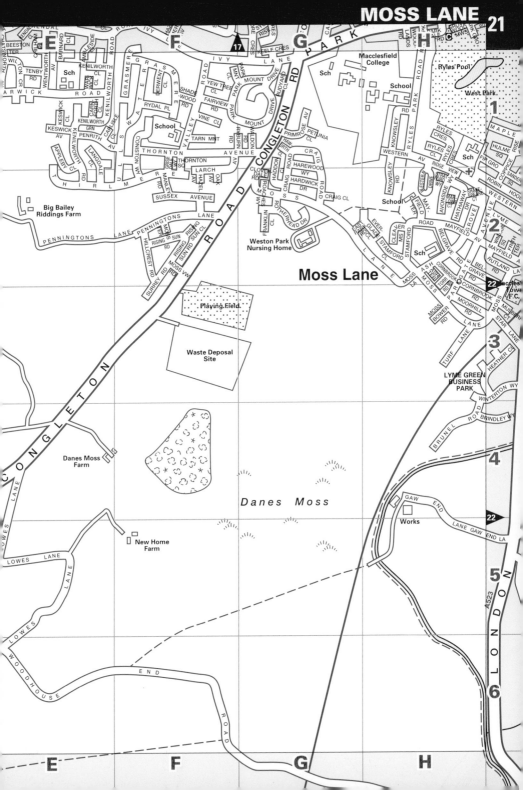

Moss Lane

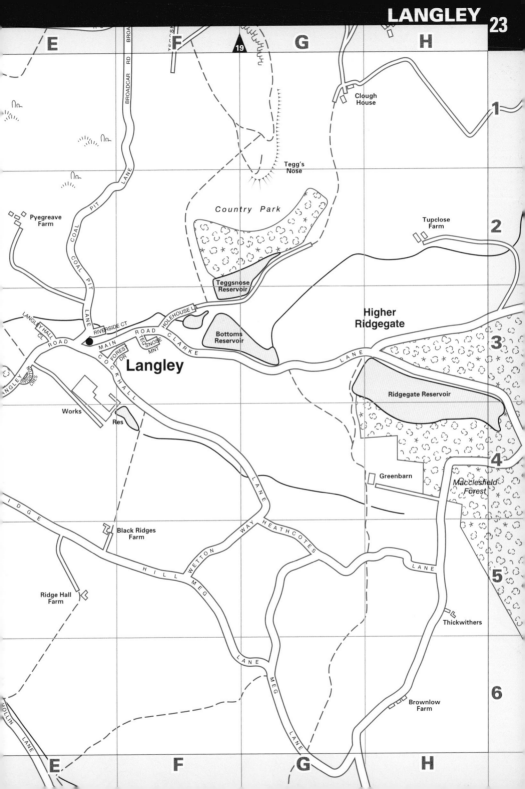

E   F   G   H

1

2

3

4

5

6

E   F   G   H

BROADCAR RD

TEGG'S N

19

Clough House

Tegg's Nose

Country Park

Tupclose Farm

Pyegreave Farm

COAL PIT LANE

Teggsnose Reservoir

Higher Ridgegate

RIVERSIDE CT

HOLEHOUSE LN

Bottoms Reservoir

CLARKE LANE

Ridgegate Reservoir

LANGLEY HALL CL

ROAD

MAIN ROAD

COCKHALL LANE

FOREST DR

SNOSE MNT

Langley

Works

Res

LANGLEY BROOK

Macclesfield Forest

Greenbarn

RIDGE HILL

Black Ridges Farm

WETTON WAY

MEG LANE

HEATHCOTES

LANE

LANE

Ridge Hall Farm

Thickwithers

MEG LANE

Brownlow Farm

MOLLIN LANE

1 **2** **3** **4**

F

A54 ROAD

Buglawton Hall School

BUXTON

ROAD

Wood Farm

Macclesfield Canal

E

Bath Vale

Buglawton

HARLEY ROAD

MARDALE CL

LINDALE AV

LEIGH RD

DAVIDSON AV

PIRIE RD

PIRIE RD

PIRIE RD

ASH AV

TALL AV

HIGH LOWE

BAILEY CRES

BEATY CRESCENT

BAILEY DRIVE

Timbers Brook Works

D

CORFIELD

SWALEDALE AV

WHARFDALE RD

LINDALE AV

WHARFDALE RD

RIBBLESDALE AV

FOSTER DRIVE

JOHN ST

HAVANNAH

CAMPBELL DRIVE

SEMPER RD

DYMOND

CRES

OLD BUXTON ROAD

Sch

School

MALHAMDALE ROAD

AVENUE

LITTLEDALE

CLAYTON AV

BANKHOUSE

HAWORTH

St JOHNS

ST JOHNS RD

FERN ST

OLD BUXTON ROAD

WILLIAM ST

C

A536 ROAD

HAVANNAH LANE

River Dane

HANCOCK RD

CRAIG RD

SOUTH RD

HAVANNAH RD

BUXTON ST

TOMMY'S LANE

B

MACCLESFIELD

Eaton Cottage Farm

LANE

Moss Farm

Cattle Market

School

DANESIDE BUSINESS PARK

INDEST

EATON BANK

EATON RD

YARBY RD

SUNSET

JACKSON

DEVON CL

ESSEX CL

WILTSHIRE DR

NORFOLK ROAD

RIVERSIDE

DANE ROW

BRIDGE ST

MILL ST

QUEEN ST

Works

BROOK ST

BRUNSWICK ST

HERBERT ST

CROWN ST

COOPER ST

BRADWELL RD

CORONATION RD

BOROUGH RD

WILBRAHAM RD

VAUDREY

SHAKERLEY RD

FERN CRESCENT

CRESCENT

HUTTON

AVEN

WESTON

EDINBURGH

Congleton Park

A

A34

MANCHESTER RD

MOSS RD

MANCHESTER ROAD

Lower Heath

GIANTSWOOD

TIDNOCK AV

MARTON AV

TIDNOCK AV

WALFIELD AV

DAISY BANK

DAISY BANK

SCOTT CL

SUFFOLK CL

SOMERSET

BERKSHIRE

LOWER HEATH LANE

RUTLAND AV

DORSET CL

WELLINGTON DRIVE

KENT DR

WOOD-

HILL

NORBURY CRES

CRES

EDLAND

HAMPSHIRE ST

MILL

MILL GREEN RD

PARK LANE

Westlow Mere

ROOD HILL

RIVERSIDE & MEADOWSIDE

FOUNDRY

WILLOW ST

MOUNTBATTEN WAY

MOOR

THE MEADOWS

KINSEY ST

FESTIVAL

RETAIL PARK

Sch

A34 BY PASS

1 **2** **26** **3** **4**

Dane in Shaw
Mossley
Congleton
BIDDULPH ROAD
A527
LANE
Staffordshire Way
Macclesfield Canal
Golf Course
Club House
Mossley Hall
Mill
School
Hosp
Rec Grnd
Cemy
The Homestead
Upper Hulme Farm
Brook House Farm
Swing-bridge
The Howty
BROOKHOUSE LANE
WARDS LA
MILL LANE
CASTLE INN RD
EDGE VIEW RD
COPPER HILL RD
CONGLETON EDGE ROAD
READES LANE
BOUNDARY LANE
MAXWELL RD
CROSSLANDS
CROSS LA
LEEK ROAD
MOSS ROAD
MOSS LANE
PEEL LANE
DODDS LANE
GORSE LA
LAMBERTS LANE
HOWEY HILL
HOWEY LANE
TUDOR WAY
PRIORY CL
DOREEN AV
ABBOTTS CL
ROSEVILLE DR
TRINITY PL
AYRSHIRE WAY
GUERNSEY CL
PARK LANE
CANAL STREET
THAMES CL
BOLLIN DRIVE
DAVEN ROAD
WOLSTANTON

The Index includes some names for which there is insufficient space on the maps. These names are preceded by an * and are followed by the nearest adjoining thoroughfare.

CONGLETON

Ullswater Rd CW12 26 B3
Union Cl CW12 24 A4
Union St CW12 24 A3

Vale Walk CW12 25 A5
Varey Rd CW12 24 B3
Vaudrey Cres CW12 24 C4
Vernon Av CW12 25 C6

Wagg St CW12 25 A5
Waggs Rd CW12 26 D5
Walfield Av CW12 24 A2
Walgrave Cl CW12 26 B2
Wallworths Bank CW12 25 B5
Walnut Rise CW12 26 C3
Wards La CW12 25 F6
Wellington Cl CW12 24 A3
Wensleydale Av CW12 24 D2
Wesley Ct CW12 25 A5
West Rd CW12 26 C3
West St CW12 26 D3
Westend Cotts CW12 26 D3
Westville Dr CW12 26 B3
Wharfdale Rd CW12 24 D2
Wharfe Cl CW12 25 C6
Wilbraham Rd CW12 24 C4
William St CW12 24 D3
Willow St CW12 24 B4
Wiltshire Dr CW12 24 A4
Windermere Dr CW12 26 B4
Windsor Pl CW12 25 C5
Wolstanholme Cl CW12 25 C6
Wood St CW12 24 A3
Woodland Av CW12 24 A4
Woodland Pk CW12 26 D3
Woolston Av CW12 24 C4
Worrall St CW12 24 A4
Worsley Dr CW12 25 E6

MACCLESFIELD

Abbey Rd SK10 17 G2
Abbotts Cl SK10 17 G2
Abingdon Cl SK11 17 F4
Acton Pl SK11 17 E5
Adelaide St SK10 18 B4
Adlington Rd SK10 14 C2
Adlington St SK10 3 A2
Adshead Ct SK10 15 E3
Albert Rd SK10 14 B3
Albert St SK11 3 A2
Alderley Rd,
Mottram St Andrew SK10 12 A1
Alderley Rd,
Prestbury SK10 16 C1
Alderley Walk SK11 3 F4
Alderney Cl SK11 17 E4
Aldersway SK10 13 E4
Alison Dr SK10 18 C4
Allen St,
Bollington SK10 15 E3
Allen St,
Macclesfield SK11 3 E3
Alma Cl SK11 17 F5
Alton Dr SK10 18 B3
Alveston Cl SK10 17 E3
Amberley Rd SK11 17 F4
Ambleside Cl SK11 21 E1
Amersham Cl SK11 17 H2
Anderson St SK10 3 B2
Andertons La SK10,11 16 B4
Andrew Gro SK10 18 D5
Angus Walk SK10 17 E2
Appleby Cl SK11 21 E1
April Rise SK10 17 F4
Arbour Cl SK10 18 A1
Arbour Cres SK10 18 A1
Arbour Mews SK10 18 A1
Archer Cl SK10 14 B4
Ardenbrook Rise SK10 13 E4
Argyll Cl SK10 17 F4
Arley Cl SK11 17 F6
Arlington Dr SK11 17 F5
Armitt St SK11 3 B4
Arundel Cl SK10 18 C3
Ascot Cl SK10 17 H2
Ash Gro SK11 21 H2
Ash Ter SK11 21 H2
Ashbourne Mews SK10 17 E4
Ashbrook St SK11 13 F5
Ashbrook Rd SK10 14 C3
Ashfield St SK10 17 F3
Ashton Av SK10 16 C4
Ashtree Cl SK10 13 H3
Astule St SK11 17 G6
Athey St SK11 3 B3
Atholl Cl SK11 17 F4
Augusta Dr SK10 17 G1
Avon Cl SK10 17 F3

Avonside Way SK11 21 H2
Aylesbury Cl SK10 18 A2

Back Eddisbury Rd SK10 19 F5
Back Paradise St SK11 3 B3
Back Wall Gate SK11 3 C2
Badger Rd,
Macclesfield SK10 18 A2
Badger Rd,
Prestbury SK10 13 F3
Baker St SK11 3 A4
Ball La SK10 14 A5
Balliol Cl SK11 22 C4
Balmoral Cres SK10 18 B3
Bamford Cl SK10 14 D3
Bamford St SK10 18 B4
Banbury Cl SK10 18 B2
Bank Cl SK11 3 F3
Bank St SK11 3 E4
Barber St SK11 3 E4
Barnard Cl SK11 21 E1
Barnett St SK11 17 G5
Barnfield Rd SK10 14 B4
Barnside Way SK10 17 H1
Barracks La SK10 18 C5
Barracks Sq SK11 3 A4
Barton St SK11 3 B4
Batemill Cl SK10 17 F3
Bearhurst La SK11 20 A2
Becks La SK10 17 E3
Bedford Rd SK11 17 G6
Beech Farm Rd SK10 18 A3
Beech Gro SK11 22 B1
Beech Hall Dr SK10 17 H2
Beech La SK10 18 A3
Beechway SK10 14 D3
Beechwood Mews SK10 17 H3
Beeston Brow SK10 14 D2
Beeston Cl SK10 15 E2
Beeston Mount SK10 15 E2
Beeston Ter SK11 17 E6
Belfry Dr SK10 13 H6
Belgrave Rd SK11 21 H2
Bell Av SK11 22 C4
Bell Farm Ct SK10 17 H1
Belmont Av SK10 16 C4
Benbrook Way SK11 20 D5
Berkshire Cl SK10 17 E3
Berristall La SK10 19 G1
Berristall Rise SK10 15 E1
Berwick Cl SK10 17 E2
Beswick St SK11 3 A3
Betchworth Way SK10 13 H6
Beverley Way SK10 17 H1
Bibbys La SK10 18 D3
Birch Av SK10 17 G4
Birches Croft Dr SK10 17 E4
Birchgate Cl SK10 17 E3
Birchinall Cl SK11 17 F6
Birchway,
Bollington SK10 14 D3
Birchway,
Prestbury SK10 13 E5
Birkdale Cl SK10 13 H6
Birtles La SK10 16 A1
Birtles Rd SK10 16 C3
Bishop Rd SK10 14 D3
Bishopton Dr SK11 17 E4
Bittern Gro SK10 17 F4
Black La SK10 3 E1
Black Rd SK11 3 F4
Blackhurst Brow SK10 12 B1
Blackley St SK10 13 H6
Blackshaw St SK11 3 B4
Blairgowrie Dr SK10 17 H1
Blakelow Bank SK11 18 C6
Blakelow Gdns SK11 18 C6
Blakelow Rd SK11 18 C6
Blandford Dr SK11 17 E4
Blaze Hill SK10 15 F2
Blenheim Cl SK10 17 F4
Bluebell Cl SK10 18 A1
Bluebell La SK10 18 A1
Bluebell Mews SK10 18 A2
Blyth Cl SK10 16 D3
Boden St SK11 3 D2
Bodmin Av SK10 16 D4
Bollin Cl SK11 3 D2
Bollin Gro SK10 13 F3
Bollin Hill SK10 13 F5
Bollin Mews,
Macclesfield SK11 22 A1
Bollin Mews,
Prestbury SK10 13 F4
Bollin Way SK10 13 F5
Bollinbarn Dr SK10 17 G2
Bollinbrook Rd SK10 17 G3
Bollington Rd SK10 14 A5
Bond St SK11 3 B4
Bonis Hall La SK10 13 F1
Boothby St SK11 3 A2

Bostock Rd SK11 17 E6
Box Tree Mews SK11 17 F5
Bracken Cl SK10 17 E4
Bradley St SK11 3 F4
Braeside Cl SK11 18 B6
Bramble Cl SK10 17 G2
Brampton Av SK10 17 F3
Bransdale Way SK11 17 E6
Bread St SK11 3 A4
Briarwood Av SK11 22 A1
Bridge End Dr SK10 13 F3
Bridge End La SK10 13 F4
Bridge Grn SK10 13 F4
Bridge St SK11 3 B3
Brighton Cres SK11 23 E3
Brindley Way SK11 21 H4
Broad Walk SK10 13 F5
Broadcar Rd SK11 19 F6
Brock St SK10 3 C1
Brocklehurst Av SK10 18 B4
Brocklehurst Ct SK10 18 A1
Brocklehurst Dr SK10 13 F3
Brocklehurst Way SK10 18 A1
Bromley Rd SK10 16 D5
Brook St SK11 3 D3
Brookfield La SK11 3 F3
Brookhouse Cl SK10 17 G3
Brooklands Av SK11 17 G6
Brooklands Mews SK11 17 G6
Brookside Cl SK11 22 C4
Brough St West SK11 3 A4
Brown St SK11 3 B3
Brunel Rd SK11 21 H4
Brunswick Hill SK10 3 D1
Brunswick St SK10 3 D1
Brunswick Ter SK10 3 D1
Brynmore Dr SK11 18 C5
Brynton Cl SK10 17 H3
Brynton Rd SK10 17 H3
Buckden Way SK10 3 A1
Buckfast Cl SK10 17 G3
Buckley St SK11 3 C4
Bucklow Walk SK11 3 A4
Bullhill La SK10 19 G2
Bullocks La SK11 22 B4
Burgess St SK10 18 C5
Butley Cl SK10 18 A1
Butley Lanes SK10 13 E1
Buxton New Rd SK10 19 E5
Buxton Old Rd SK11 18 D6
Buxton Rd SK10 3 D2
Byron Cl SK11 22 A1
Byrons La SK11 22 B1

Calamine St SK11 18 B6
Calder St SK11 14 C3
Calrofold La SK10 19 E3
Calveley Rd SK10 17 F4
Camborne Av SK10 16 D4
Cambridge Av SK11 17 G6
Cambridge Rd SK11 17 G6
Campbell Cl SK10 17 F3
Canal Side SK11 3 F4
Canal St SK10 3 E2
Canton St SK11 22 A1
Canton Walks SK11 22 A1
Capesthorne Way SK11 18 C6
Cardigan Cl SK11 17 F5
Carisbrook Av SK10 18 B3
Carlisle Cl SK11 21 E1
Carnegie Cl SK10 17 F3
Carnforth Cl SK11 21 E1
Carnoustie Dr SK10 14 A6
Cartmel Cl SK10 17 G2
Castle Hill SK10 12 D4
Castle Hill Ct SK10 13 E4
Castle Rise SK10 13 E4
Castle St SK11 3 C2
Castleford Dr SK10 12 D4
Castlegate SK10 13 E4
Castlegate Mews SK10 13 E4
Castletown Cl SK10 13 H6
Catherine St SK11 3 B2
Cavendish Cl SK10 18 A2
Cedar Gro SK11 22 A2
Cedarway SK10 13 F4
Chadwick Ter SK10 18 B3
Chancery La SK10 14 D3
Chantry Ct SK11 22 A2
Chapel La SK10 15 G6
Chapel St,
Bollington SK10 15 E2
Chapel St,
Macclesfield SK11 3 D3
Charity La SK11 19 H5
Charlotte St SK11 3 D3
Charlotte St West SK11 3 C2
Charlton St SK11 3 A2
Charnwood Cl SK11 17 F4
Charter Rd SK10 14 D3
Charter Way SK10 18 B2
Chatham St SK11 3 C2
Chatsworth Av SK11 17 E6

Chelford Rd,
Henbury SK11 16 A5
Chelford Rd,
Prestbury SK10 12 A5
Cherington Cres SK11 17 G6
Cherryfields Rd SK11 17 E5
Cheshire Vw SK10 15 E4
Chester Rd SK11 3 A2
Chestergate SK11 3 B2
Chestnut Av SK10 18 B3
Chestnut Cl SK10 18 B3
Cheveley Cl SK10 17 H2
Chilham Pl SK11 21 E1
Chiltern Av SK11 17 F6
Cholmondeley St SK11 3 C4
Church La,
Henbury SK11 16 B4
Church La,
Rainow SK10 15 G6
Church La, Sutton Lane Ends SK11 17 H1
Church La, Warren SK11 20 C5
Church Mews SK10 14 D2
Church St West SK11 3 C2
Church St,
Bollington SK10 15 E2
Church St,
Macclesfield SK11 3 C3
Church Way SK10 17 E2
Churchill Way SK11 3 C1
Churchside SK10 3 D2
Clare Dr SK10 17 H2
Clarence Rd SK10 14 D2
Clarence Ter SK10 14 D1
Clarendon Dr SK10 18 C4
Clarke La,
Bollington SK10 14 A5
Clarke La,
Langley SK11 23 F3
Clarke Ter SK11 22 A1
Cleaver Mews SK11 21 H2
Clegg St SK10 3 E3
Clevedon Cl SK11 17 F6
Cliff La SK10 18 D3
Clifford Rd SK11 17 F5
Clough Bank SK10 14 C4
Cloverdale Rd SK11 21 G2
Clowes St SK11 17 G5
Coachway SK10 13 F3
Coal Pit La SK11 23 E2
Coare St SK10 3 B1
Cockhall La SK11 23 E3
Cocksheadhey Rd SK10 15 E1
Collar House Dr SK10 12 D5
Collingwood Cl SK10 17 G2
Colville Rd SK11 17 E5
Commercial Rd SK10 3 D1
Congleton Rd SK11 20 C6
Coniston Way SK11 21 F1
Consort Cl SK10 14 B4
Conway Cres SK10 18 C3
Coope Rd SK10 14 B4
Cop Mdw SK11 22 C4
Copper St SK11 3 F4
Coppice Rise SK11 22 A2
Cornbrook Rd SK11 21 H2
Cornfield Cl SK10 17 H1
Cornwall Cl SK10 17 E3
Coronation St SK11 22 A1
Corporation St SK10 18 B4
Cotswold Cl SK11 16 D3
Cottage La SK10 18 C5
Cottage St SK11 3 A2
Countess Cl SK11 17 F6
Countess Rd SK11 17 E6
Cow La,
Bollington SK10 15 E3
Cow La,
Macclesfield SK11 22 A1
Craig Cl SK11 21 G2
Craig Rd SK11 21 G1
Cranford Av SK11 18 C6
Crew Av SK10 18 B4
Crompton Rd SK11 3 A2
Crookedyard Rd SK11 19 H6
Cross St SK11 22 A1
Crossall St SK11 3 B3
Crossfield Rd SK10 14 B4
Crown St West SK11 3 A3
Cuckstool Pit Hill SK10 3 F2
Cumberland St SK10 15 E3
Cumberland St SK10 3 A2
Cundiff Cl SK11 3 F4

Daintry St SK11 3 E3
Daintry Ter SK10 3 E3
Daisy Bank SK11 18 B6
Dale Head Rd SK10 13 F6
Dale St SK10 3 E2
Dalesford Cres SK10 17 E4
Danes Sq SK11 22 A2

Dark La, Henbury SK11 16 A
Dark La, Warren SK11 20 A
Dawson Rd,
Bollington SK10 14 D
Dawson Rd,
Macclesfield SK11 17 E
Dean Cl SK10 14 D
Deerwood Cl SK10 17 E
Delamere Dr SK10 18 C
Derwent Cl SK11 21 F
Devon Cl SK10 17 E
Dingle Cl SK10 17 G
Donagh Cl SK10 17 E
Dorchester Way SK10 13 H
*Dorset Walk,
Durham St SK11 17 E
Dover Rd SK10 18 C
Downes Cl SK10 17 F
Downing Cl SK11 22 C
Drummond Way SK10 16 D
Dudley Walk SK11 17 E
Duke St SK11 3 C
Dukes Ct SK11 3 C
Dumbah La SK10 14 A
Dunster Rd SK10 17 E
Durham Cl SK10 17 E

Eaglais Way SK10 17 E
Earlsway SK11 17 E
East Av SK10 14 B
East Park Rd SK11 21 G
Eaton La SK11 22 A
Ecton Av SK10 18 D
Eddisbury Cl SK11 18 C
Eddisbury Ter SK11 18 C
Eden Rd SK10 18 C
Edgeway SK11 16 B
Edinburgh Dr SK10 17 F
Edward St SK11 17 G
Eldon Rd SK10 17 E
Elgin Av SK10 17 F
Elizabeth House SK11 3 F
Elizabeth St SK11 3 C
Elm Dr SK10 18 B
Elm Rise SK10 12 D
Elmsway SK10 14 D
Endon Av SK10 14 C
*Essex Walk,
Hereford Cl SK11 17 E
Everglade Cl SK11 21 H
Evesham Cl SK10 18 B
Exchange Cl SK11 3 C
Exchange St SK11 3 C

Fairfield Av SK10 14 D
Fairhaven Cl SK10 13 G
Fairview Rd SK11 21 F
Fallibroome Cl SK10 17 E
Fallibroome Rd SK11 17 E
Falmouth Cl SK10 16 D
Farfields Cl SK11 20 D
Farmfield Dr SK10 17 H
Farnham Av SK11 17 F
Farwood Cl SK10 17 F
Fearndown Way SK10 17 H
Fence Av SK10 3 E
Fern Bank Rise SK10 14 D
Fern Lea Bank SK11 17 H
Ferndale Cres SK10 16 D
Field Cl SK10 14 C
Field View Dr SK11 22 B
Fieldbank Rd SK11 17 G
Fir Ct SK10 17 E
Fir Gro SK11 21 H
Fitz Cl SK10 18 A
Fitz Cres SK10 18 A
Fitzwilliam Av SK11 22 C
Flash La SK10 14 A
Flint St SK10 3 E
Foden St SK10 18 A
Folkestone Cl SK10 17 G
Forest Cl SK10 15 G
Forest Dr SK11 23 E
Forge Cl SK11 20 D
Foundry Ct SK11 3 B
Foundry St SK10 3 E
Fountain St SK10 3 E
Fowey Cl SK10 16 C
Fowler St SK10 18 A
Foxglove Cl SK10 15 E
Frances St SK11 17 G
Franklin Cl SK11 21 G
Freshfield Dr SK10 17 H
Friars Cl SK10 15 G
Friars Way SK10 17 E
Frith Ter SK11 22 A
Fytton Cl SK11 20 C

Garden St,
Bollington SK10 14 C
Garden St,
Macclesfield SK10 3 E
Gas Rd SK10 3 D

aw End La SK11 21 H5
awsworth Rd SK11 16 D6
eorge St SK11 3 D3
eorge St West SK11 3 B2
ilchrist Av SK11 17 E6
leave Av SK10 14 D3
leneagles Dr SK10 13 H6
loucester Cl SK10 18 B1
oathland Way SK11 22 A1
onville Av SK11 22 C3
oodall St SK11 3 E3
oodwood Cl SK11 22 B1
osling St SK10 3 E2
range Rd SK11 3 B4
rangelands SK10 17 E2
rapes St SK11 3 D4
rasmere SK11 21 F1
reat King St SK11 3 A2
reat Queen St SK11 3 B2
reen Hills Cl SK11 3 F4
reen La SK10 15 E2
reen Mdws SK11 17 F6
reen St SK10 3 E3
reenbank Dr SK10 14 D2
reendale La SK10 12 D3
reenfield Rd SK10 14 D3
reengates SK10 17 E3
reg Av SK10 14 B3
reyhound Rd SK10 12 A6
reystoke Rd SK10 18 B3
rimshaw Av SK10 14 D3
rimshaw La SK10 14 C3
risedale Way SK11 21 F1
rosvenor Centre SK11 3 C2
rosvenor St SK10 3 B1
rovewood Mews SK11 3 B4
ullane Cl SK10 17 G1
unco La, Butley Town SK10 13 H2
unco La, Macclesfield SK11 22 B1

addon Cl SK11 21 G2
alf St SK11 22 A1
all Cl SK10 18 A1
all Gro SK10 18 A1
all Hill SK10 14 B3
all La SK11 22 C3
all St SK10 3 A2
allefield Cres SK11 3 F3
allefield Dr SK11 3 E3
allefield Rd SK11 3 E3
amble Way SK10 16 D3
amilton Cl SK10 18 D5
*Hampshire Walk, Durham Cl SK10 17 E3
and St SK11 3 A2
ardwick Dr SK11 21 G2
arewood Way SK11 21 G1
arper Cl SK11 18 A6
arrington Dr SK11 20 C6
arrop Rd SK10 15 E2
arrops Pl SK11 3 A4
artley Grn SK10 14 B3
arvest Rd SK10 17 H2
athaway Dr SK11 21 H2
atton Brow Ter SK11 22 C3
atton St SK11 3 B4
aughton Cl SK10 17 F4
awkins La SK10 19 F2
aworth Cl SK11 21 G1
awthorn Rd SK10 14 C3
awthorn Rise SK10 12 D4
awthorn Way SK10 18 B2
ayfield. Cl SK10 17 G1
ayle Cl SK10 16 C4
azel Av SK11 21 F2
azelhurst Dr SK10 14 D2
azelmere Av SK11 17 F6
eapy St SK11 3 E4
eath Rd SK10 14 B4
eathcotes La SK11 23 G5
eather Cl SK11 22 A3
edgerow SK10 15 F2
edingham Cl SK10 17 F4
enbury Rise SK11 16 B5
enderson St SK11 3 B3
enley Cl SK10 13 H6
enshall Rd SK10 14 B3
ereford Cl SK10 17 E3
ewetson Cres SK11 17 E6
eybridge La SK10 13 G3
eyes Farm Rd SK11 17 E5
ibel Rd SK10 3 C1
*Higginbotham Grn, Old Mill La SK11 22 B1
igh Ct SK10 14 D2
igh St, Bollington SK10 15 E3
igh St, Macclesfield SK11 3 D4
igher Fence Rd SK10 18 C3

Higher La SK10 14 D4
Highfield SK10 13 F6
Highfield Dr SK10 17 G3
Highfield Rd, Bollington SK10 14 D3
Highfield Rd, Macclesfield SK11 3 A3
Hightree Dr SK11 16 B4
Hill Cl SK10 17 G1
Hill St SK11 3 C4
Hill Vw SK10 14 C4
Hillcrest Rd, Bollington SK10 14 B3
Hillcrest Rd, Macclesfield SK11 21 F2
Hillside Ct SK10 18 D3
Hillside Dr SK10 18 D3
Hilton Cl SK11 17 E6
Hobson St SK11 3 C4
Holehouse La, Bollington SK10 13 H1
Holehouse La, Macclesfield SK11 23 F3
Holland St SK11 3 B3
Hollands Pl SK11 3 F3
Hollin La SK11 22 C4
Hollin Rd SK10 14 C4
Hollins Rd SK11 18 B6
Hollins Ter SK11 18 C6
Holly Rd SK11 17 G5
Holmlee Way SK10 12 C4
Home Farm Av SK10 17 E4
Hope St SK10 3 E2
Hope St West SK10 3 A1
Horseshoe Dr SK11 3 A3
Hough Cl SK10 15 G5
Houghley Cl SK10 17 H2
Howe St SK10 18 C3
Hulley Pl SK10 18 C3
Hulley Rd SK10 18 B2
Hulme Sq SK11 22 A1
Hurdsfield Rd SK10 3 D1
Hurst La SK10 14 D2
Huxley Cl SK10 17 G3

INDUSTRIAL ESTATES:
East Tytherington Business Pk SK10 14 A6
Fence Av Industrial Est SK10 3 F1
Hurdsfield Business Centre SK10 18 C2
Hurdsfield Industrial Est SK10 18 B2
Lyme Grn Business Pk SK1 21 H3
Silk Rd Retail Pk SK10 18 B2

Ingersley Rd SK10 15 E2
Irwell Rise SK10 14 C3
Ivy La SK11 17 F6
Ivy Rd SK11 17 F6
Ivymeade Cl SK11 17 E6
Ivymeade Rd SK11 17 E6

Jackson La SK10 14 D3
Jackson St SK11 22 A1
James St SK11 3 C4
Jarman Rd SK11 22 C3
Jodrell Cl SK11 3 E3
Jodrell St SK11 3 E3
John St SK10 14 D2
Johns Cl SK10 15 G5
Jordangate SK10 3 C1
Judy La SK11 22 C4
Jumper La SK10 15 H5
Juniper Rise SK10 16 D3
Justice St SK10 18 A3

Keats Dr SK10 17 E3
Keele Cres SK11 21 G1
Kempton Way SK10 13 H6
Kendal Cl SK11 17 E6
Kendal Rd SK11 17 E6
Kenilworth Cl SK11 21 E1
Kenilworth Grn SK11 21 E1
Kenilworth Rd SK11 21 E1
Kennedy Av SK10 17 E3
Kennet Way SK11 17 E5
Kent Av SK10 14 B4
Kent Walk SK10 17 E3
Kentwell Dr SK10 17 H2
Kerridge Rd SK10 19 E2
Kershaw Gro SK11 17 G4
Keswick Av SK11 21 E1
Keswick Cl SK11 21 E1
King Edward Rd SK10 3 C1
King Edward St SK10 3 B1
Kings Walk SK10 18 B5
Kingston Av SK11 18 C6
Kingsway SK10 14 B4
Kirkstall Cl SK10 17 G3

Knight St SK11 3 E4
Knights Cl SK11 3 E4
Knowsley Rd SK11 21 H1
Knutsford Walk SK11 3 F4

Laburnum Rd SK11 22 B1
Lakelands Cl SK10 18 C5
Lanark Walk SK10 17 E2
Landseer Dr SK10 17 E4
Langdale Cl SK11 21 E1
Langford St SK11 3 A2
Langley Hall Cl SK11 23 E3
Langley Rd SK11 22 D4
Lanreath Cl SK10 16 C4
Lansdowne St SK10 18 B4
Larch Av SK11 21 F2
Lark Hall Cl SK10 18 D5
Lark Hall Cres SK10 18 D5
Lark Hall Rd SK10 18 D5
Lathom Way SK10 18 C3
Lavenham Cl SK10 17 H2
Lea Bank Cl SK11 17 F5
Leadbeaters Cl SK11 18 C6
Leadbeaters Rd SK11 18 C6
Leamington Rd SK10 17 E4
Ledley St SK10 14 C3
Leek Old Rd SK11 22 B4
Legh Rd SK10 13 F3
Leigh St SK11 3 E3
Lidgetts La SK10 19 E1
Lilford Sq SK11 22 A2
Lime Gro SK10 3 F2
Lincoln Cl SK10 15 G5
Lincoln Pl SK10 17 E2
*Lincoln Walk, Lincoln Pl SK10 17 E2
Lincombe Hey SK10 13 H3
Lindrick Cl SK10 13 H6
Lindrum Av SK11 22 A4
*Lingdale Walk, White St SK11 22 A1
Lingfield Cl SK10 17 H1
Linnet Gro SK10 17 F3
Little Aston Cl SK10 17 H1
Little Meadow Cl SK10 13 G4
Little St SK10 3 C1
Livingstone Cl SK10 17 E4
Lodge Brow SK10 14 C1
Lomas Sq SK11 22 A2
London Rd Ter SK11 22 A2
London Rd, Macclesfield SK11 22 A2
London Rd, Prestbury SK10 13 G1
Loney St SK11 3 A3
Long La SK10 15 E1
Longacre St SK10 3 A2
Longbutts La SK11 20 D5
Longden La SK11 18 D6
Longden St SK10 3 F3
Lord St, Bollington SK10 15 E3
Lord St, Macclesfield SK11 3 D4
Lowe St SK11 3 D3
Lower Bank St SK11 3 E4
Lower Exchange St SK11 3 D2
Lowerfield Rd SK10 18 B3
Lowes La SK11 21 E5
Lowther St SK10 15 E2
Loxley Cl SK11 3 A3
Ludlow Cl SK10 18 B3
Lumley Rd SK11 17 E6
Lutyens Cl SK10 17 E4
Lyme Av SK11 22 A2
Lyme Grn Settlement SK11 22 A5
Lyme Vw SK11 22 A5
Lynn Gro SK11 3 A4
Lyon St SK11 3 B3

Macclesfield Rd, Over Alderley SK10 12 A6
Macclesfield Rd, Prestbury SK10 13 E6
Madron Av SK10 16 D4
Maggoty La SK11 20 C6
Magnolia Rise SK10 12 D4
Maidstone Cl SK10 17 G2
Main Rd SK11 23 E3
Malvern Dr SK10 14 B6
Manchester Rd SK10 18 A1
Manley Rd SK11 21 F2
Manor Cres SK10 18 A2
Maple Av SK11 22 A1
Marigold Cl SK11 17 E5
Market Pl, Bollington SK10 15 E2
Market Pl, Macclesfield SK10 3 C1
Marl Edge SK10 13 F6
Marlborough Cl SK10 14 A6

Marlborough Ct SK11 3 D3
Marlborough Dr SK10 18 A1
Marlowe Ct SK11 21 H2
Marsden Ter SK11 3 B3
Marton Cl SK10 17 E4
Marton La SK11 20 A5
Masons La SK10 18 B3
Maxfield Cl SK10 17 E4
Mayfield Av SK11 21 H2
Mayfield Ter SK11 21 H2
Meadow Dr SK10 13 G4
Meadow Way SK10 18 B3
Meadowside SK11 3 B2
Meadway SK10 13 F5
Mee St SK11 22 B1
Meg La, Macclesfield SK10 16 D4
Meg La, Sutton SK11 23 F5
Melford Dr SK10 17 H2
Melksham Cl SK11 17 G6
Merebrook Cl SK11 17 F5
Merebrook Rd SK11 17 E5
Mereside Cl SK11 17 F3
Merriden Rd SK10 17 G3
Merrydale Cl SK10 17 E3
Middlehills SK11 18 D6
Mill Cotts SK10 15 E2
Mill La, Bollington SK10 15 E3
Mill La, Macclesfield SK11 3 D4
Mill Rd SK11 18 A6
Mill St SK11 3 C2
Millbank Dr SK10 17 E3
Millers Mdw SK10 15 G5
*Millstone Passage, Old Mill La SK11 22 B1
Minor Av SK11 22 A4
Monsall Cl SK11 18 C5
Monsall Dr SK11 18 C6
Montrose Cl SK10 17 F4
Moorhill Rd SK11 21 H3
Moorlands Cl SK10 17 H1
Moran Cres SK11 3 A4
Moran Rd SK11 3 A4
Morton Dr SK11 22 C4
Moss Bower Rd SK11 21 H3
Moss Brow SK10 14 B3
Moss La, Bollington SK10 14 A3
Moss La, Macclesfield SK11 21 G2
Moss La, Mottram St Andrew SK10 12 A1
Moss Sq SK11 22 A2
Moss Ter SK11 21 F2
Moss View Rd SK11 21 F2
Mount Pleasant SK10 15 E2
Mount Ter SK11 18 C5
Muirfield Dr SK10 14 A6
Mulberry Ct SK11 22 A3
Murray Cl SK10 17 F3
Murrayfield SK10 13 F6

Nab Cl SK10 15 F1
Nab La SK10 15 E1
Nancy Vw SK10 15 E3
Needhams Wharf Cl SK10 18 C3
Nelson St SK11 3 C4
Nether Fold SK10 13 F3
New Hall St SK10 17 H4
New Rd SK10 13 F4
Newgate SK11 3 C3
Newham Cl SK11 22 C3
Newlands Rd SK10 16 D5
Newlyn Av SK10 16 D4
Newquay Dr SK10 16 D4
Newton St SK11 3 B4
Nicholson Av SK10 18 B3
Nicholson Cl SK10 18 B3
Nixon St SK11 17 G5
Norbury St SK11 3 A3
*Norfolk Walk, Stafford Cl SK10 17 E2
Northgate Av SK10 17 H4
Northmead SK10 13 F5
Nursery Rd SK10 14 B4

Oak Av SK11 21 F2
Oak Bank Dr SK10 15 E2
Oak La SK10 14 D5
Oak Rd SK10 12 A1
Oakenbank La SK10 15 F2
Oakhill Cl SK10 17 G1
Oakwood Dr SK10 13 H4
Old Farm Cl SK10 17 F3
Old Hall St SK10 18 A4
Old Mill La SK11 22 B1
Oldham St SK10 15 E2
Oldhams Rise SK10 18 A1
Oliver Cl SK10 14 B3
Orme Cl, Macclesfield SK10 18 A1
Orme Cl, Prestbury SK10 13 F3
Orme Cres SK10 18 A1
Ovenhouse La SK10 14 B4
Oxford Rd SK11 3 A3
Oxney Cl SK10 17 F4

Packsaddle Pk SK10 12 D5
Paddock Brow SK10 13 F5
Padstow Cl SK10 16 D4
Palmerston Rd SK11 17 F5
Palmerston St SK10 14 D2
Paradise St SK11 3 B3
Park Brook Rd SK11 17 F5
Park Grn SK11 3 D3
Park Gro SK11 3 B4
Park House Dr SK10 13 F2
Park House La SK10 13 F2
Park La SK11 3 A4
Park Mount Cl SK11 21 F1
Park Mount Dr SK11 21 F1
Park Royal Dr SK11 3 A2
Park St, Bollington SK10 15 E2
Park St, Macclesfield SK11 3 D4
Park Vale Rd SK11 17 H6
Park Vw SK10 3 E1
Parker St SK11 3 E3
Parkett Heyes Rd SK11 17 E5
Parkgate Av SK11 21 H3
Parr St SK11 3 A3
Parsonage St SK11 3 D4
Parvey La SK11 22 B5
Pasture Cl SK10 17 H2
Pavilion Way SK10 17 E4
Pearl St SK10 13 F4
Pearle St SK10 3 C1
Pearson St SK11 3 F3
Pedley Hill SK10 15 G6
Peel St SK11 3 C4
Pembroke Rd SK11 17 E5
Penningtons La SK11 21 F2
Penny La SK10 19 F2
Penrith Av SK11 21 E1
Penzance Cl SK10 16 D4
Pepper St SK11 16 B5
Peter St SK11 3 A3
Peter St West SK11 3 A3
Peterborough Cl SK10 17 F3
Peterhouse Rd SK11 22 C3
Peters Cl SK10 13 F3
Petunia Cl SK11 21 G1
Peveril Walk SK11 17 E5
Pexhill Dr SK10 16 D5
Pexhill Rd SK10,11 16 C6
Pickenham Cl SK11 17 E6
Pickford St SK11 3 D3
Pierce St SK11 3 B2
Pine Cl SK10 18 C4
Pine Hurst SK10 13 E4
Pine Rd SK10 18 C4
Pinfold St SK11 3 B2
Pitt St SK11 22 A1
Pleasant St SK10 18 C3
Ploughmans Way SK10 17 G1
Polperro Cl SK10 16 D4
Pool End Cl SK10 14 A6
Pool End Rd SK10 14 A6
Pool St SK11 3 E4
Poplar Gro SK10 14 D2
Poplar Rd SK11 3 C4
Portford Cl SK10 17 E3
Portland Walk SK11 17 E6
Portmarnock Cl SK10 17 G1
Portrush Dr SK10 17 H1
Pownall Sq SK11 3 A2
Pownall St SK10 3 C1
Poynton St SK10 3 A2
Prestbury La SK10 13 G3
Prestbury Rd, Macclesfield SK10 3 A1
Prestbury Rd, Over Alderley SK10 12 A5
Preston St West SK11 3 A4
Prestwick Cl SK10 13 H6
Priest La SK10 12 A1
Primrose Av SK11 21 G1
Princes Way SK11 17 E5
Princess Dr SK10 14 B4
Princess St SK10 14 C3
Priory Dr SK10 17 E3
Priory La SK10 17 E3
Pumptree Mews SK11 16 D5

Quayside Way SK11 3 F4
Queen St, Bollington SK10 15 E2
Queen St, Macclesfield SK10 3 D1
Queen Victoria St SK11 3 D2

Queens Av SK10 18 B3
Queens Cl,
  Bollington SK10 14 B4
Queens Cl,
  Macclesfield SK10 18 B2

Raglan Rd SK10 18 C3
Rainow Rd SK10 18 D3
Rainow Vw SK10 15 E2
Ravenhoe La SK10 19 G1
Rayleigh Way SK10 17 E3
Redruth Av SK10 16 D4
Redway La SK10 15 E4
Regent Av SK11 17 G6
Renfrew Cl SK10 17 E4
Richmond Hill SK11 22 B1
Richmond Pl SK11 22 B1
Ridge Hill SK11 22 D4
Ridge Vw SK11 21 H1
Ridley Rd SK10 14 B3
Riseley St SK10 3 A1
Rising Sun Cl SK11 21 F2
Rising Sun Rd SK11 21 F2
River St SK11 3 E4
Riverbank Cl SK10 14 C3
Riverside Ct SK11 23 E3
Riverside Dr SK10 13 F5
Roaches Way SK11 21 G2
Roan Ct SK11 3 F3
Roan House Way SK11 3 F3
Roan Mews SK11 3 F3
Robin Cres SK11 22 A4
Robin Hood Av SK11 22 A2
Robin La SK11 22 A5
Robins Cl SK10 15 G5
Robins Way SK10 14 D3
Rodney St SK11 3 C4
Roe St SK11 3 C3
Roewood La SK10 14 C3
Rose Bank SK10 14 C3
Rose Way SK11 22 A1
Rotherhead Dr SK11 21 G2
Rough Heys La SK11 16 A5
Round Gdns SK10 14 D2
Round Mdw SK10 15 G6
Rowan Way SK10 18 B3
Rowanside SK10 12 D4
Roxburgh Cl SK10 17 F4
Royal Mdws SK10 17 F4
Rudyard Cl SK11 21 G1
Rugby Cl SK10 18 B1
Rugby Dr SK10 18 B2
Rushton Fold SK10 12 A1
Rutland Rd SK11 22 A2
Ryburn Rd SK11 21 F1
Rydal Pl SK11 21 F1
Ryebank Way SK10 17 H2
Ryle St SK11 3 C4
Ryles Cl SK11 21 H1
Ryles Cres SK11 21 H1
Ryles Park Rd SK11 21 H1

Saddleback Dr SK10 13 E4
Saddlers Way SK11 19 G6
St Andrews Rd SK11 3 A4
St Austell Av SK10 16 C4
St Austell Cl SK10 17 E4
*St Barnabas Ct,
  White St SK11 22 A1
*St Edwards Cl,
  White St SK11 22 A1
St Georges Pl SK11 3 D4
St Georges St SK11 3 D4
St Ives Cl SK10 17 E4
St James Av SK11 20 D5
St Johns Rd SK11 3 C3
St Pauls Rd SK11 3 E3
Salisbury Pl SK10 18 B1
*Salop Walk,
  Wiltshire Cl SK10 17 E2
Samuel St SK11 3 C3
Sanders Sq SK11 22 A2
Sandgate Rd SK10 18 C2
Sandown Pl SK11 17 E6
Sandringham Rd
  SK10 18 C4
Sandwich Dr SK10 17 H1
Sandy Cl SK10 14 C4
Sandy La SK10 16 B3
Saville St SK11 3 F4
School La SK11 16 A6
School La SK11 20 A1
Scott Cl SK10 18 D5
Scott Hope Cl SK11 17 E2
Scott Rd SK11 13 F3
Selkirk Cl SK10 17 E2
Selwyn Dr SK11 22 C3
Sevenoaks Cl SK10 17 G3
Severn Cl SK10 17 F3
Shadewood Rd SK11 21 F1
Shakespeare Ct SK11 21 H2
Sharpley St SK10 3 A2
Shaw St SK11 3 B2

Shaws La SK10 12 B3
Shelbourne Mews
  SK10 17 E4
Sherbourne Rd SK11 17 E6
Sherwood Rd SK11 22 A2
Shirleys Cl SK10 13 F4
Shirleys Dr SK10 13 F4
Short St SK11 3 D2
Shrigley Rd SK10 15 E2
Shrigley Rise SK10 15 E2
Shrigley St SK10 3 E2
Silvan Ct SK10 17 G3
Silver St SK10 15 E2
Simpsons Ct SK11 3 B2
Slack St SK11 22 B1
Slater St SK11 3 A4
Smith St SK11 22 A1
Smithy Brow SK10 15 F2
Smithy La SK10 12 B1
Snape Rd SK10 18 B2
Snow Hill SK11 22 B1
Somerton Cl SK11 17 E6
Somerton Rd SK11 17 E6
South Acre Dr SK11 18 C6
South Down Cl SK10 18 A1
South Park Rd SK11 3 B4
South St SK11 22 A1
South View Av SK11 20 C5
South West Av SK10 14 B3
Southfield SK11 13 F6
Sowcar Way SK10 15 E2
Spencer Brook SK10 13 E4
Spinners Way SK10 14 C3
Spinney Mead SK10 18 B3
Spring Gdns SK10 18 A3
Springbank SK10 14 B3
Springfield Rd SK11 17 E5
Springfields SK10 13 F3
Springhill SK10 18 D3
Springwood Way SK10 14 A5
Spuley La SK10 15 F1
*Square St,
  Cross St SK11 22 B1
Squirrels Chase SK10 13 F6
Stafford Cl SK10 17 E2
*Stafford Walk,
  Stafford Cl SK10 17 E2
Stamford Cl SK11 21 H2
*Stamford Ct,
  Stamford Rd SK11 21 H2
Stamford Rd SK11 21 H2
Stanley St SK11 3 C2
Stapleton Rd SK10 17 G3
Star La SK11 22 A3
Statham St SK11 3 C4
Station St SK10 18 A4
Steeple St SK10 3 E1
Step Hill SK11 3 D2
Stevenage Cl SK11 3 A3
Stevenage St SK11 3 A3
Stirling Cl SK10 17 E2
Stocks La SK11 15 G5
Stoneleigh Cl SK10 17 H3
Stoneyfold La SK11 18 D6
Store St SK10 15 E2
Stratford Way SK11 21 H2
Stuart Ct SK11 17 G2
Stubbs Ter SK11 3 E4
Suffolk Cl SK10 17 E3
Sugar La SK10 15 G5
Summerhill Rd SK10 17 E1
Sunderland St SK11 3 D3
Sunningdale Rd SK11 17 F6
Sunnybank Cl SK11 22 A2
Surrey Rd SK11 21 F3
Sussex Av SK11 21 F2
Sutherland Dr SK11 17 F3
Sutton Cl SK11 22 A2
Swallow Cl SK10 18 C5
Swanscoe Av SK10 14 C4
Swettenham St SK11 3 F3
Swiss Cott SK10 17 G3
Sycamore Cres SK11 17 G6
Sycamore Rise SK11 17 G6
Symondley Rd SK11 22 C5

Tabor St SK11 3 F4
Tamar Cl SK10 16 D3
Tarn Mount SK11 21 F1
Tarvin Cl SK11 22 B2
Taylors Sq SK11 3 A4
Teggsnose La SK11 19 F6
Tegsnose Mount SK11 23 F3
Telford Cl SK11 18 C4
Tenby Rd SK11 21 E1
Tennyson Cl SK11 16 D6
Tewkesbury Dr SK10 14 B6
The Crescent SK11 18 B4
The Fold SK10 13 F2
The Paddocks SK10 13 F6
The Silk Rd,
  Bollington SK10 14 A5
The Silk Rd,

Macclesfield SK10 3 D1
The Village SK10 13 E4
The Whitfields SK10 17 F4
Thetford SK10 17 H2
Thirlmere SK11 21 E2
Thistleton Cl SK11 22 A1
Thorne Cl SK10 13 F6
Thornton Av SK11 21 F1
Thornton Sq SK11 21 F1
Thornway SK10 14 D3
Thornycroft Cl SK11 20 D5
Thornycroft St SK11 3 E3
Thorp St SK10 3 D1
Timber St SK10 18 C3
Tintagel Cl SK10 16 D4
Toll Bar Av SK11 18 C5
Toll Bar Rd SK11 17 E5
Tonbridge Cl SK10 17 G2
Torr Rd SK11 21 H3
Tower Hill SK11 19 G1
Townley Pl SK11 3 D3
Townley St SK11 3 D3
Treen Cl SK10 16 D4
Trinity La SK11 22 C4
Trinity Sq SK10 18 B4
Truro Cl SK10 16 D4
Tudor Dr SK10 12 D4
Tunnnicliffe Rd SK11 22 B4
Turf La SK11 21 H3
Turnberry Cl SK10 13 H6
Turner Rise SK10 15 E2
Turner St SK10 15 E2
Turnock St SK11 3 E3
Tynedale Cl SK11 3 A2
Tytherington Dr SK10 18 A1
Tytherington Grn SK10 13 H6
Tytherington La SK10 14 A6
Tytherington Park Rd
  SK10 18 A2

Ullswater SK11 21 F2
Underwood Cl SK10 17 E3
Unicorn Gate Way SK10 3 D1
Union Rd SK11 3 F3
Union St SK11 3 B3

Valley Rd SK11 21 F1
Vernon St SK10 3 F2
Vicarage Way SK11 17 E5
Victoria Rd SK10 3 A1
Vincent St SK11 3 C4
Vine Cl SK11 21 F1
Vine St SK10 15 E2

Waldon Rd SK11 21 G1
Walker La SK11 22 B4
Walker St SK10 3 A1
Waller St SK11 3 D4
Walton Heath Dr SK10 13 H6
Ward Av SK10 14 D3
Wardle Cres SK11 20 D6
Wardle St SK11 3 C3
Wardour Cl SK11 17 E6
Warren Dr SK11 20 D6
Warren Gro SK11 20 D5
Warwick Cl SK11 21 E1
Warwick Rd SK11 21 E1
Water St,
  Bollington SK10 14 D2
Water St,
  Macclesfield SK11 3 C3
Waterhouse Av SK10 14 C3
Waterloo St West SK11 3 B2
Watermill Dr SK11 18 C5
Waters Grn SK11 3 D2
Waterside SK11 3 E4
Waverley Cl SK11 18 D5
Wayside Rd SK10 18 C5
Weavers Ct SK11 3 A3
Well La,
  Butley Town SK10 13 H2
Well La, Rainow SK10 15 H2
Wellesbourne Cl SK10 17 E4
Wellington Rd SK10 14 C3
Wellington St SK11 3 C3
Wenlock St SK10 17 G3
Wentworth Av SK11 21 E1
West Bank Rd SK11 17 G4
West Bond St SK11 3 A3
West Cl SK10 14 C3
West House Ct SK10 16 D4
West St SK11 17 G5
Westbrook Dr SK10 17 H3
Westbury Dr SK11 17 G5
Westerham Cl SK10 17 G3
Western Av SK11 21 H1
Western Av SK11 22 A2
Western Dr SK11 21 H2
Westfields Av SK10 17 G3
Westminster Rd SK10 3 B1
Westminster St SK11 3 C1
Westmorland Cl SK10 17 E3

Wetheral Rd SK11 17 G2
Wetton Way SK11 23 F5
Weybridge Dr SK10 17 H1
Whalley Hayes SK10 3 B1
Wheatfield Cl SK10 17 H2
Whirley La SK10 16 A3
Whirley Rd SK10 16 B3
Whiston St SK11 3 B3
White St SK11 22 A1
Whitney Cft SK10 18 C4
Willerby Cl SK10 3 A1
William St SK10 3 F2
Williams Way SK11 16 B4
Willow Bank Dr SK10 15 E2
Willow Ct SK10 17 G2
*Willow Mews,
  Suffolk Cl SK10 17 E3
Willow Way SK10 13 F5
Willowmead Dr SK10 13 F6
Wilmslow Old Rd
  SK10 12 A1
Wilmslow Rd SK10 12 B1
Wilmslow Walk SK10 13 E4
Wilton Cres SK11 21 E1
Wiltshire Cl SK10 17 E2
*Wiltshire Walk,
  Wiltshire Cl SK10 17 E2
Wilwick La SK11 17 E5
Windmill La SK11 15 E4
Windmill St SK11 3 D4
Windsor Cl SK10 14 B4
Windsor Sq SK11 22 A2
Winterton Way SK11 21 H3
Withinlee Rd SK10 12 B5
Withyfold Dr SK10 18 A3
Woburn Cl SK10 17 H3
Wood St SK11 3 D3
Woodhouse End Rd
  SK11 21 E6
Woodhouse La SK11 20 D5
Woodlands Rd SK11 3 A4
Woodlea Dr SK10 14 B2
Woodstock Cl SK10 17 E3
Worthington Cl SK11 16 B4
Wren Cl SK10 17 F3
Wrigley La SK10 16 A1
Wykeham Chase SK11 17 F6

Yew Tree Cl,
  Macclesfield SK11 21 F1
Yew Tree Cl,
  Prestbury SK10 13 G3
Yew Tree Way SK10 13 H4
York Ct SK10 3 E2
York St SK10 3 E2

POYNTON

Abbotsbury Cl SK12 4 C2
Adams Cl SK12 4 D5
Adlington Cl SK12 5 E5
Adlington Pk SK12 4 B6
Alder Av SK12 5 E4
Alderley Cl SK12 5 F6
Anglesey Dr SK12 5 E1
Anglesey Water SK12 5 E1
Anson Rd SK12 5 G3
Arlington Dr SK12 4 C4
Ash Rd SK12 5 E4

Bagstock Av SK12 4 D5
Balmoral Dr SK12 4 C4
Barclay Av SK12 5 E5
Bardell Cres SK12 4 C5
Barnaby Rd SK12 4 C5
Beech Cres SK12 5 E3
Birch Rd SK12 5 E5
Bittern Cl SK12 4 A4
Blenheim Cl SK12 5 E3
Bolton Cl SK12 4 C3
Bosley Dr SK12 5 F5
Brecon Cl SK12 5 E4
Brent Cl SK12 4 A3
*Brook Cotts,
  Clumber Rd SK12 4 D4
Brookfield Av SK12 4 C4
Brookside Av SK12 4 D4
Brownlow Cl SK12 4 D5
Buckfast Cl SK12 4 D3
Buckingham Rd SK12 4 D4
Bulkeley Rd SK12 4 D4
Burton Dr SK12 4 D3
Bylands Cl SK12 4 C3

Calder Cl SK12 4 D6
Capenhurst Cl SK12 5 E3
Carleton Rd SK12 5 H3
Cedar Cl SK12 5 E4
Charlecote Rd SK12 5 E3
Cherry Tree Av SK12 5 E4
Chester Rd SK12 4 A3

Chestnut Dr SK12 5 E
Clifford Rd SK12 4 C
Clumber Cl SK12 4 D
Clumber Rd SK12 4 D
Collingwood Cl SK12 5 F
Copperfield Rd SK12 4 D
Coppice Rd SK12 5 F
Correction Brow SK12 5 H
Covell Rd SK12 4 D
Curzon Rd SK12 4 C

Dale House Fold SK12 5 F
Derbyshire Rd SK12 5 H
Deva Cl SK12 4 B
Dickens La SK12 4 D
Distaff Rd SK12 4 D
Dombey Rd SK12 4 D
Dorrit Cl SK12 4 D
Dundrennan Cl SK12 4 C
Dunlin Cl SK12 4 C

Easby Cl SK12 4 C
Eaton Cl SK12 5 F
Elm Beds Rd SK12 5 E
Elm Cl SK12 5 E

Fielding Av SK12 4 D
Fir Cl SK12 4 C
First Av SK12 4 C
Fountains Cl SK12 4 C
Fulmar Cl SK12 4 A
Furness Cl SK12 4 A

Gawsworth Rd SK12 5 E
Georges Cl SK12 4 D
Georges Rd East SK12 4 D
Georges Rd West SK12 4 D
Glastonbury Dr SK12 4 C
Glenfield Dr SK12 4 C
Gloucester Rd SK12 4 C
Graymarsh Dr SK12 4 D
Grebe Cl SK12 4 A
Green La SK12 5 H
Grosvenor Dr SK12 4 C
Gull Cl SK12 4 A

Hale Av SK12 4 D
Hardwicke Rd SK12 5 E
Hartland Cl SK12 4 C
Haseley Cl SK12 4 D
Hawthorn Gro SK12 4 C
Hazel Dr SK12 5 E
Hazelbadge Cl SK12 4 C
Hazelbadge Rd SK12 4 C
Hepley Rd SK12 5 H
Heron Dr SK12 4 A
Highfield Rd SK12 4 D
Hilton Gro SK12 4 D
Hilton Rd SK12 5 H
Hockley Cl SK12 5 F
Hockley Rd SK12 5 F
Holker Cl SK12 5 E
Holly Rd SK12 4 D
Hope Green Way SK10 4 C
Hope La SK10 4 C

INDUSTRIAL ESTATES:
Adlington Industrial Est
  SK12 4 B
Ivy Rd SK12 5 E

Kettleshulme Way SK12 5 F
Kingswood SK12 4 C
Kirkstall Cl SK12 4 C
Knole Cl SK12 5 E

Ladys Cl SK12 4 D
Lady's Incline SK12 5 E
Lakeside Dr SK12 5 E
Lambourn Cl SK12 4 C
Larch Cl SK12 5 F
Lawrence Pl SK12 4 C
Legh Cl SK12 4 D
Lindisfarne Dr SK12 4 C
London Rd North SK12 4 C
London Rd South SK12 4 C
Long Row SK12 4 C
Lostock Av SK12 4 A
Lostock Hall Rd SK12 4 C
Lostock Rd SK12 4 C
Lower Park Cres SK12 5 H
Lower Park Rd SK12 4 B
Lyme Rd SK12 5 H

Mallard Cres SK12 4 A
Malmesbury Cl SK12 4 C
Maple Av SK12 5 E
Marley Rd SK12 5 F
Mayfair Cl SK12 4 D
Meadway SK12 4 A
Melrose Cres SK12 5 H
Merton Cl SK12 4 A
Micawber Rd SK12 4

iddlewood Rd SK12 5 F4
ill Hill Av SK12 4 C1
ill Hill Hollow SK12 4 C1
illstone Cl SK12 5 E2
ilton Dr SK12 4 C3
loreton Dr SK12 5 E3

arrow La SK10 5 F6
eath Cl SK12 4 C2
elson Dr SK12 5 F4
elson Cl SK12 5 F5
ewstead Cl SK12 4 C2
ickleby Rd SK12 4 D4
ursery Dr SK12 4 C4

ak Gro SK12 4 C3
akfield Rd SK12 5 E3
rchard Cl SK12 5 E4

addock Chase SK12 5 E1
ark Av SK12 4 D3
ark La SK12 4 D4
arklands Way SK12 4 A4
ckwick Rd SK12 4 A4
ne Rd SK12 5 F4
ochard Dr SK12 4 A3
ool House Rd SK12 5 H2
rince Rd SK12 5 H3
rinces Incline SK12 5 H3
uffin Av SK12 4 A4

ueensway SK12 4 C4
Queensway Ho,
 Queensway SK12 4 C4

agley Cl SK12 5 E3
ainow Dr SK12 5 F5
edacre SK12 5 E1

t Elmo Pk SK12 5 H3
andringham Dr SK12 5 H3
chool Cl SK12 5 E3
chool La SK12 5 E3
econd Av SK12 4 C6
elby Cl SK12 4 C3
heldon Rd SK12 5 H5
hrigley Rd North
 SK12 5 H5
hrigley Rd South SK12 5 H5
iddington Rd SK12 5 F5
nipe Cl SK12 4 A4
outh Mead SK12 4 A3
outh Park Dr SK12 4 D3
oenlow Cl SK12 4 D6
oinners La SK12 4 B3
oring Rd SK12 5 E5
typerson Way SK12 4 D4
ulgrave Av SK12 5 E3
utton Rd SK12 5 F5
wan Cl SK12 4 A4

apley Av SK12 4 D5
eal Av SK12 4 A3
arren Dr SK12 4 A3
ewkesbury Cl SK12 4 C3
hird Av SK12 4 C6
intern Cl SK12 4 D2
ower Gdns SK12 5 E2
owers Cl SK12 5 E2
owers Rd SK12 5 E1
rafalgar Av SK12 5 F4
rafalgar Cl SK12 5 F4
ulworth Rd SK12 4 D3

arden Rd SK12 4 D5
ernon Cl SK12 4 D5
ernon Rd SK12 4 C5
icarage La SK12 4 D2

Warford Av SK12 5 F5
Warren Cl SK12 4 A3
Warren Lea SK12 5 E3
aterloo Rd SK12 5 F6
aters Reach SK12 5 E2
ayside Dr SK12 4 B3
eller Av SK12 4 D5
eller Cl SK12 4 C5
est Park Av SK12 4 A3
hitby Cl SK12 4 C3
idgeon Cl SK12 4 A3
igwam Cl SK12 4 C3
illow Cl SK12 5 E4
incle Av SK12 5 F5
indsor Cl SK12 5 E4
oburn Ct SK12 5 F4
ood La North SK10 5 G6
oodford Rd SK12 4 A3
oodside SK12 4 D3
oolley Av SK12 4 C5

ew Tree La SK12 5 E5

Yew Tree Rd SK10 5 G6

WILMSLOW

Acacia Av SK9 8 B4
Adlington Rd SK9 9 F3
Albany Rd SK9 8 B4
Albert Rd SK9 8 C3
Alderdale Gro SK9 8 A4
Alderley Lodge SK9 8 C4
Alderley Rd,
 Mottram St Andrew
 SK10 11 G2
Alderley Rd,
 Wilmslow SK9 8 C6
Aldford Pl SK9 10 B1
Alma La SK9 8 C3
Alton Rd SK9 8 B2
Altrincham Rd,
 Styal SK9 6 A3
Altrincham Rd,
 Styal SK9 9 E1
Alveston Dr SK9 9 E1
Anderton Way SK9 7 H6
Annis Cl SK9 10 D1
Annis Rd SK9 10 D1
Anson Rd SK9 7 G6
*Appleton Walk,
 Lyngard Cl SK9 7 G6
Apprentice La SK9 6 B4
Arclid Cl SK9 7 G6
Arkle Av SK9 7 G3
Arlington Cres SK9 8 A4
Arlington Way SK9 8 A4
Artists La SK10 10 C5
Ash Gro SK9 7 E4
Ashberry Cl SK9 9 F1
Ashbrook Rd SK10 11 H6
Ashcroft Cl SK9 7 H5
Ashdene Rd SK9 8 B5
Ashford Cl SK9 7 F3
Ashford Rd SK9 8 C5
Ashley Rd SK9 8 D6
*Aston Way,
 Spath La SK9 7 G2
Avondale Rise SK9 9 F4

Balmoral Way SK9 8 D3
Bankside Cl SK9 7 F5
Barford Dr SK9 7 F6
Barlow Rd SK9 8 D6
Barton Cl SK9 7 G5
Beaufort Chase SK9 7 H6
Beaufort Cl SK9 10 D1
Beaumont Cl SK9 7 E2
Beddells La SK9 8 C3
Beech Cl SK9 8 D6
Beech Cotts SK9 10 C3
Beech Gro SK9 8 C3
Beech La SK9 8 C3
Beech Rd SK9 10 D1
Beechfield Av SK9 8 B4
Beechfield Rd SK9 10 C3
Beechway SK9 8 C4
Beechwood Dr SK9 9 G1
Beeston Rd SK9 7 G2
Belfry Cl SK9 9 F1
*Benbrook Gro,
 Foden Walk SK9 7 F6
Benson Walk SK9 7 F5
Berry Cl SK9 8 D4
Bidston Dr SK9 7 G5
Birch Av SK9 8 C3
Birchwood Dr SK9 9 F2
Birtles Way SK9 7 G1
*Blackden Walk,
 Shrigley Cl SK9 7 F6
Blackshaw La SK9 10 B3
Blenheim Cl SK9 9 F2
Bluebell Way SK9 7 E6
Bolleyn Wood Cl SK9 7 E6
Bollin Ct SK9 9 F3
Bollin Hill SK9 8 D1
Bollin Walk SK9 9 E2
Bollinwood Chase SK9 9 F2
Bolshaw Farm La SK8 7 E1
Bolshaw Rd SK8 7 E1
Booth Rd SK9 6 C6
Bosden Cl SK9 7 F2
Bosley Cl SK9 7 F5
Bourne St SK9 8 C3
Bowery Av SK8 7 H1
Brackenwood Mews
 SK9 9 G1
Bradford La SK10 10 C6
Bramley Cl SK9 8 A5
Brandon Cl SK9 7 F5
Brereton Rd SK9 7 G4
Briarwood SK9 9 E2
Brick La SK9 8 A4
Bridge Dr SK9 7 F4
Bridgefield Av SK9 7 E6

Brindley Gro SK9 7 G5
Broad Walk SK9 8 B1
Broadway SK9 8 D3
Brook La SK9 8 A6
Brooke Av SK9 7 F3
Brooke Dr SK9 7 F3
Brooke Way SK9 7 G3
Brookside Ter SK9 8 A6
Broomfield Cl SK9 9 G1
Brown St SK9 10 C2
Browns La SK9 8 B1
Buckingham Rd SK9 8 B3
Budworth Walk SK9 7 G6
Bulkeley Rd SK9 7 E4
Burford Cl SK9 8 B4
Burford Cres SK9 8 A4
Burnside Cl SK9 8 C3

Caldy Rd SK9 7 F4
Calverley Cl SK9 9 E1
Cambridge Av SK9 8 B3
Campden Way SK9 7 F3
Capesthorne Rd SK9 8 B5
Cardenbrook Gro SK9 9 G1
Carlisle St SK9 10 C3
Carlton Av SK9 7 E5
Carnoustie Cl SK9 9 F1
Carr Mill Mews SK9 6 D6
Carrs Cl SK9 8 D2
Carrwood Rd SK9 8 B1
Cavendish Mews SK9 8 D4
Cedarway SK9 8 C5
Chadwick Cl SK9 9 E1
Chancel La SK9 8 D1
Chapel Ct SK9 8 C3
Chapel La SK9 8 B3
Chapel Rd SK9 10 C2
Chapel St SK9 10 C2
Chatsworth Rd SK9 8 A5
*Chelford Ct,
 Chelford Rd SK9 7 G2
Chelford Rd,
 Alderley Edge SK9 10 A3
Chelford Rd,
 Handforth SK9 7 G2
Chelston Dr SK8 7 E1
Cherington Cl SK9 7 H4
Cherry Tree Cl SK9 9 G1
Chesham Cl SK9 8 B5
Chesham Rd SK9 8 B6
Chester Cl SK9 7 G6
Chestnut Cl SK9 9 G1
Chorley Hall Cl SK9 10 B2
Chorley Hall La SK9 10 B2
*Christleton,
 Spath La SK9 7 G2
Church Av SK9 6 C5
Church Cl SK9 7 F4
Church La SK9 10 C1
Church Rd,
 Handforth SK9 7 F3
Church Rd,
 Wilmslow SK9 8 B6
Church St SK9 8 D2
Church Ter SK9 7 F3
Church Vw SK9 6 C5
Church Walk SK9 8 C3
Clare Av SK9 7 E4
Clarence Ct SK9 8 D3
Clay La SK9 7 E3
Cliff Rd SK9 8 D1
Cliff Side SK9 8 D1
*Cliffbrook Gro,
 Bosley Cl SK9 7 F5
Clifford Rd SK9 8 C3
Clifton Rd SK9 8 B5
Clifton St SK9 10 C2
Clough Av SK9 7 E5
Cobbetts Way SK9 8 C5
College Cl SK9 8 B1
Colshaw Dr SK9 7 F6
Colshaw Walk SK9 7 F6
Commercial Av SK8 7 G2
Congleton Cl SK9 10 C3
Congleton Rd SK9 10 C3
Coniston Dr SK9 7 E3
Connaught Cl SK9 9 F1
Constable Dr SK9 9 G1
Copperfields SK9 9 E1
Coppice Way SK9 7 G3
Corner Cft SK9 8 C5
Cornwell Cl SK9 9 G1
Cottage Gro SK9 8 B4
Cottage Lawns SK9 10 C1
Countess Av SK8 7 G2
Courtney Grn SK9 7 F5
Covington Pl SK9 8 D3
Cow La SK9 9 E2
Cragside Way SK9 9 E3
*Cranage Way,
 Spath La SK9 7 G2
Cranford Rd SK9 6 C6
Crescent Rd SK9 10 D1

Croft Rd SK9 8 B5
Crofters Grn SK9 8 B3
Croftside Way SK9 9 E3
Cross La SK9 9 H1
Crossfield Rd SK9 7 F4
Croston Cl SK9 11 E3
*Crowbrook Gro,
 Wheelock Cl SK9 7 F6
*Cuddington Way,
 Pickmere Cl SK9 7 F2
Cumber Cl SK9 8 A5
Cumber Dr SK9 8 A5
Cumber La SK9 8 A4
Curzon Mews SK9 8 C4
*Dairybrook Gro,
 Lyngard Cl SK9 7 G6

Dane Dr SK9 9 F3
Daresbury Cl SK9 9 F1
Davenham Av SK9 8 C2
Davenham Rd SK9 7 G3
Davenport Av SK9 8 A5
Davey La SK9 10 C1
Daveylands SK9 9 F3
Davies Av SK9 7 E1
Dean Cl SK9 7 F6
Dean Dr SK9 7 F5
Dean Rd SK9 7 G4
Dean Row Rd SK9 7 E6
Deanway SK9 7 E6
Delamere Rd SK9 7 F3
Denewood Ct SK9 8 C3
Derwent Dr SK9 7 F2
Devonshire Dr SK9 10 D2
Dingle Av SK9 8 A6
*Dinglebrook Gro,
 Malpas Cl SK9 7 G6
Donkey La SK9 8 C4
Dorac Av SK9 7 E1
Dorchester Cl SK9 9 F1
Downesway SK9 10 B3
Draxford Ct SK9 8 D3
Drayton Cl SK9 7 F6
Duke Av SK8 7 H1
Duke St SK9 10 D1
Dunham Rd SK9 7 F2

Earl Rd SK8 7 G2
Eastham Way SK9 7 F2
Eastward Av SK9 8 B3
Eaton Dr SK9 10 B1
*Eccleston Way,
 Henbury Rd SK9 7 G2
Eden Cl SK9 8 B4
Edgehill Chase SK9 9 G2
Edgeway SK9 8 D4
*Edleston Gro,
 Picton Dr SK9 7 F6
Egerton Rd SK9 6 D6
Elderberry Way SK9 9 G1
Elm Cres SK9 10 D1
Elm Gro,
 Alderley Edge SK9 10 C1
Elm Gro,
 Handforth SK9 7 E4
*Elmfield Cl,
 Elmfield Rd SK9 10 C1
Elmfield Rd SK9 10 C1
Elton Cl SK9 7 G6
Elworth Way SK9 7 G3
Epsom Av SK9 7 G3
Evesham Dr SK9 7 E5

Fair Lawn Cl SK9 7 G6
Fairbourne Av,
 Alderley Edge SK9 8 D6
Fairbourne Av,
 Wilmslow SK9 8 B5
Fairbourne Cl SK9 8 B5
Fairbourne Dr SK9 8 B5
Fairfax Dr SK9 8 B5
Fairford Way SK9 9 F2
Fawns Keep SK9 9 F2
Ferndale SK9 7 F4
Fernwood Gro SK9 9 E1
Festival Dr SK10 11 H5
Fieldhead Mews SK9 9 G1
Fieldhead Rd SK9 9 G1
Finlow Hill La SK10 11 F5
Finney Cl SK9 7 E5
Finney Dr SK9 7 F5
Fletsand Rd SK9 9 E3
Foden Walk SK9 7 F5
Friars Cl SK9 8 B1
Frodsham Way SK9 7 G3
Fulmards Cl SK9 9 E2
Fulshaw Av SK9 8 C3
Fulshaw Cl SK9 8 C4
Fulshaw Pk SK9 8 C4
Fulshaw Pk South SK9 8 C5

Gable Av SK9 8 C2
Gail Cl SK9 10 D1

Gainsborough Cl SK9 9 F1
Garth Heights SK9 9 E2
Gatcombe Mews SK9 8 D3
Gawsworth Way SK9 7 G3
George St SK9 10 C2
Gladewood Cl SK9 9 E1
Gleneagles Cl SK9 9 F1
Glenside Dr SK9 9 E3
Goodrington Rd SK9 7 G4
Goostrey Cl SK9 7 G6
Gorsefield Hey SK9 9 G1
Gorsey Rd SK9 8 B2
Gowy Cl SK9 7 G6
Grange Park Av SK9 8 C1
Grangeway SK9 7 F3
Granville Rd SK9 8 B4
Grasmere Rd SK9 10 C2
Grason Av SK9 7 E6
Gravel La SK9 8 A5
Greaves Rd SK9 8 B2
Green Dr SK9 7 F5
Green Hall Mews SK9 8 D3
Green La,
 Alderley Edge SK9 10 B3
Green La,
 Wilmslow SK9 8 D3
Green St SK9 10 C2
Green Villa Pk SK9 8 A5
Greenhythe Rd SK8 7 E1
Greenway SK9 8 D3
Greenway Rd SK8 7 E1
Greenwood Dr SK9 9 F1
Greg Mews SK9 7 E5
Greta Av SK9 7 E1
Greystoke Dr SK9 10 C1
Grosvenor Cl SK9 8 C5
*Grove Arcade,
 Grove St SK9 8 D2
Grove Av SK9 8 D2
Grove St SK9 8 D2
Grove Way SK9 8 D2

Haddon Cl SK9 10 B2
Half Acre Grn SK9 9 E1
Hall Rd, Handforth SK9 7 G4
Hall Rd, Wilmslow SK9 8 C2
Hallwood Rd SK9 7 G5
Halstone Av SK9 8 A5
Hampson Cres SK9 7 E3
Handforth By-Pass SK9 7 G1
Handforth Rd SK9 7 G5
Harden Pk SK9 8 D6
Harefield Dr SK9 8 D4
Harefield Rd SK9 7 G3
Hartford Av SK9 8 B4
Hassall Way SK9 7 G2
Hawthorn Av SK9 8 C2
Hawthorn Gro SK9 8 D2
Hawthorn La SK9 8 C2
Hawthorn Rd SK9 8 D2
Hawthorn St SK9 8 C3
Hawthorn Ter SK9 8 C3
Hawthorn Vw SK9 8 D2
Hawthorn Walk SK9 8 C2
Hazelcroft Gdns SK9 10 C3
*Hazeldean Ct,
 Pinewood Rd SK9 9 G1
Hazelwood Rd SK9 9 E1
Heatherfield Ct SK9 9 G1
Heathfield SK9 8 C5
Heatley Way SK9 7 G3
Helsby Way SK9 7 F3
Henbury La SK8 7 H1
Henbury Rd SK9 7 F3
Herald Ct SK9 8 D2
Hereford Dr SK9 7 G4
Heyes La SK9 10 C2
Heywood Cl SK9 10 D1
Heywood Rd SK9 10 D1
Highfield Cres SK9 7 E6
Highfield Estate SK9 7 E6
Highgrove Mews SK9 8 C3
Hilbre Way SK9 7 G3
Hill Dr SK9 7 G4
Hill Top Av SK9 9 E1
Hocker La SK10 10 D6
Hollies La SK9 9 H2
Hollin La SK9 6 C2
Holly Bank Rd SK9 6 D6
Holly La SK9 6 A3
Holly Rd North SK9 8 D3
Holly Rd South SK9 8 D4
Holmeswood Cl SK9 9 E1
Holts La SK9 6 B4
*Hooton Way,
 Spath La SK9 7 G2
Hope Av SK9 7 F4
Horseshoe La SK9 10 C1
Hough La SK9 7 F5
Howty Cl SK9 7 F6
Hunters Cl SK9 7 H6
Hunters Mews SK9 9 F3
Hunters Vw SK9 7 E4

Huntly Chase SK9 9 F3
Hurlbote Cl SK9 7 F2
Hurstlea Ct SK9 10 C1

INDUSTRIAL ESTATES:
Deanway Business Pk
  SK9 7 F4
Handforth Dean Retail Pk
  SK9 9 E2
Riverside Pk SK9 9 E2
Stanley Green
  Industrial Est SK9 7 G2
Stanley Green Retail Pk
  SK9 7 H1

Irwin Dr SK9 7 F2

Kelsall Way SK9 7 F2
Kenilworth Av SK9 7 F2
Kennerleys La SK9 8 D2
Kennet Cl SK9 7 F5
Kensington Ct SK9 8 C3
*Kettleshulme Walk,
  Picton Dr SK9 7 G6
Kiln Croft La SK9 7 G3
Kings Cl SK9 8 D3
Kings Rd SK9 8 B1
Kingsbury Dr SK9 9 F1
Kingsley Av SK9 7 E5
Kingston Rd SK9 7 F3
Knightsbridge Cl SK9 7 F6
Knowle Grn SK9 7 E4
Knowle Pk SK9 7 E4
Knutsford Rd SK9 8 A6

Lacey Av SK9 7 E6
Lacey Cl SK9 7 E6
Lacey Ct SK9 7 E6
Lacey Grn SK9 7 E6
Lacey Gro SK9 7 E6
Ladybrook Gro SK9 7 F5
Ladyfield St SK9 9 E2
Ladyfield Ter SK9 9 E2
Lancaster Rd SK9 7 G6
Lancelyn Dr SK9 9 F1
Land La SK9 9 E4
Langley Dr SK9 7 G4
Larchwood Dr SK9 9 G1
Leafield Dr SK8 7 H1
Leaside Way SK9 9 E3
Lincoln Rd SK9 7 G6
Lindfield Est North
  SK9 8 C3
Lindfield Est South
  SK9 8 C3
Lindow La SK9 8 A3
Lindow Par SK9 8 B3
Links Rd SK9 8 B6
London Rd SK9 10 C2
Long Marl Dr SK9 7 H3
Longmeade Gdns SK9 9 E3
Longsight La SK8 7 H2
*Lostock Ct,
  Lostock Rd SK9 7 F3
Lostock Rd SK9 7 F3
Lower Meadow Rd
  SK9 7 G3
Lydiat La SK9 10 C3
Lyme Av SK9 6 D6
Lymewood Dr SK9 9 G1
Lyndhurst Cl SK9 8 A4
Lyngard Cl SK9 7 G6
Lynton Ct SK9 10 C1
Lynton La SK9 10 C1

Macclesfield Rd,
  Alderley Edge
  SK9,10 10 C2
Macclesfield Rd,
  Wilmslow SK9 9 F1
Malpas Cl SK9 7 G6
Mainwaring Dr SK9 9 F1
Manchester Rd SK9 7 E6
Manor Cl SK9 8 B1
Manor Gdns SK9 9 F2
Manor Rd SK9 8 B1
Maple Rd SK9 10 D1
Maplewood Rd SK9 9 G1
Marbury Rd SK9 8 D1
Marina Cl SK9 9 F2
Marlborough Av SK9 10 D1
Marlow Dr SK9 7 E2
Marthall Way SK9 7 G2
Marton Way SK9 7 G2

*Massey St,
  Chapel St SK9 10 C2
Mayfield Gro SK9 8 A5
Meadow Brow SK9 10 C2
Meadow Cl SK9 8 B5
Meadow Way SK9 8 B5
Meadscroft Dr SK9 10 B2
Meddings Cl SK9 10 C3
Medway Cl SK9 7 F5
Meriton Rd SK9 7 E3
Mill Rd SK9 8 D2
Mill St SK9 9 E2
Millbrook Gro SK9 7 F6
Mobberley Rd SK9 8 A1
Moor La SK9 8 A4
Moorfield Dr SK9 8 A4
*Moorsbrook Gro,
  Lyngard Cl SK9 7 G6
Moorway SK9 8 A5
Moran Cl SK9 7 G5
Moreton Dr SK9 7 G4
Moss La,
  Alderley Edge SK9 10 D2
Moss La, Styal SK9 6 A2
Moss Rd SK9 10 D1
Moss Rose SK9 10 D1
Moss Ter SK9 9 H1
Mosswood Rd SK9 9 G1
Mottram Rd SK9 10 D2
Mount Pleasant SK9 8 D1
Muirfield Cl SK9 9 F1

Nantwich Way SK9 7 G2
Neston Way SK9 7 F4
Netherfields SK9 10 C3
New St SK9 8 A4
Newgate SK9 8 A2
Newlands Dr SK9 8 A4
Newton Rd SK9 6 D6
Nightingale Cl SK9 6 D6
*Norbury Way,
  Sandiway Rd SK9 7 G2
Northfield Dr SK9 9 G1
Northward Rd SK9 8 B3
Nursery La, Nether Alderley
  SK10 10 A6
Nursery La,
  Wilmslow SK9 8 C3

Oak Cl SK9 8 B3
Oak Cotts SK9 6 B3
Oak La SK9 8 B3
Oak Mews SK9 7 E6
Oakdean Ct SK9 6 D6
Oakenclough Cl SK9 7 F5
Oakfield Cl SK9 10 D1
Oakfield Rd SK9 10 D1
Oakhurst Chase SK9 10 C1
Oaklands Cl SK9 7 G6
Oaklea Av SK9 8 C4
Oakmere Cl SK9 7 F2
Oakwood Av SK9 8 B4
Oatlands SK9 10 D3
Old Hall Cres SK9 7 G4
Old Orchard SK9 8 C2
Old Rd, Handforth SK9 7 G4
Old Rd, Wilmslow SK9 8 D1
Ollerton Rd SK9 7 G2
One Oak La SK9 9 H2
Orchard Cl SK9 8 B4
Orchard Cres SK10 10 B5
Orchard Dr SK9 7 G5
Orchard Grn SK9 10 D2
Orme St SK9 10 C2
Orwell Cl SK9 7 F5
Osborne Cl SK9 9 F3
Osprey Dr SK9 9 E1
Overhill Dr SK9 9 G2
Overhill La SK9 9 G2
Overhill Rd SK9 9 F2
Overton Way SK9 7 F2

Park Av SK9 9 E1
Park Cres SK9 6 D6
Park Rd SK9 8 C2
*Parkgate Way,
  Church Ter SK9 7 F3
Parkway SK9 8 D3
Parsonage Grn SK9 8 D3
Paxford Pl SK9 8 D4
Peacock Dr SK8 7 E1
Peacock Way SK9 7 F2
Peckhill Cl SK9 7 G6
Peover Rd SK9 7 G2

*Pickmere Ct,
  Pickmere Rd SK9 7 F2
Pickmere Rd SK9 7 F2
Picton Dr SK9 7 G6
Pinewood Rd SK9 9 G1
Plumley Rd SK9 7 F2
Poplar Av SK9 8 B4
Pownall Ct SK9 8 A1
Pownall Rd SK9 8 B1
Prescott Rd SK9 6 D6
Prestbury Rd SK10 11 H6
Prestbury Rd SK10 11 G5
Prestbury Rd,
  Prestbury SK9 9 E4
Princess Rd SK9 8 C4
Priory Rd SK9 8 B1

Quarry Bank Rd SK9 6 B4
Queen Ann Ct SK9 9 E3
Queens Rd SK9 8 C3

Racecourse Pk SK9 8 B3
Racecourse Rd SK9 8 A2
*Rainow Way,
  Malpas Cl SK9 7 G6
Ravenswood Rd SK9 8 B5
Redbrook Gro SK9 7 F6
Redesmere Cl SK9 10 B2
Redesmere Rd SK9 7 F2
Reeman Cl SK9 6 D6
Regent Bank SK9 8 C4
Regent Cl SK9 8 C4
Reynolds Mews SK9 9 G1
Richmond Av SK9 7 F2
Ridgeway SK9 9 H2
Ringstead Cl SK9 7 F6
Ringstead Dr SK9 7 F6
River St SK9 8 D1
Riverside Walk SK9 9 E2
Roan Way SK9 10 D3
Rodeheath Cl SK9 9 F2
Rodepool Cl SK9 7 F5
Rookerypool Cl SK9 7 F5
Rossenclough Rd SK9 7 F6
Rostherne Rd SK9 8 B5
Rowanside Dr SK9 9 G1
Rushside Rd SK8 7 H1
Ryleys La SK9 10 B2

Sagars Rd SK9 7 E3
St James Dr SK9 8 C3
St James Way SK8 7 H1
St Johns Rd SK9 8 A6
*Salterbrook Gro,
  Malpas Cl SK9 7 G6
Sand La SK10 10 B6
Sandhurst Dr SK9 9 F1
Sandiway Rd SK9 7 G2
Sandown Cl SK9 9 F1
Sandringham Way SK9 8 D3
Sandy La SK9 8 A1
School La SK10 11 H5
School Rd SK9 7 F4
Sealand Way SK9 7 F3
Sedgeford Cl SK9 7 F6
Sefton Cl SK9 7 E5
Sefton Dr SK9 7 E5
Shargate Cl SK9 7 E6
Shaws Fold SK9 6 C4
*Shellbrook Gro,
  Rossenclough Rd
  SK9 7 F6
Shenhurst Cl SK9 8 A5
Sherbrook Rise SK9 9 F3
Shirley Av SK8 7 E1
Shrigley Cl SK9 7 F6
Siddington Rd SK9 7 F2
Silverdale Dr SK9 8 C5
Simpson St SK9 8 C3
Slade La SK9 11 G6
Smiths Lawn SK9 8 D4
*Snapebrook Gro,
  Gowy Cl SK9 7 G6
Somerford Way SK9 7 G2
Sossmoss La SK10 10 A5
South Bank Cl SK9 10 D1
South Cl SK9 8 C3
South Gro SK9 10 C2
South Oak La SK9 8 B4
South St SK9 10 C2
South Ter SK9 10 C3
Southacre Dr SK9 7 F4
Southfield Cl SK9 7 E4
Spath La SK9 7 F2

Spinney Cl SK9 7 E4
Spring St SK9 8 D2
Springfield Dr SK9 8 A4
Squirrels Jump SK9 10 D2
Stamford Rd,
  Alderley Edge SK9 10 C2
Stamford Rd,
  Wilmslow SK9 6 D6
Stanhope Cl SK9 9 G1
Stanley Rd SK9 7 F1
Stannelands Cl SK9 7 E5
Stannelands Dr SK9 7 E5
Stannelands Rd SK9 6 D3
Station Rd,
  Handforth SK9 7 F4
Station Rd, Styal SK9 6 C4
Station Rd,
  Wilmslow SK9 9 E2
Stevens St SK9 10 C2
Stockton Rd SK9 8 C5
Stoney La SK9 8 B4
Strawberry La SK9 8 B4
Stretton Way SK9 7 F1
Styal Av SK9 7 E6
Styal Rd SK9 6 C1
Styal Rd SK9 6 C6
Suffolk Dr SK9 7 E6
Summerfield Pl SK9 8 D4
Sunbury Cl SK9 7 G5
Sunninghey Ct SK9 10 B1
Sunnybank Dr SK9 8 A5
Sutton Rd SK9 10 B2
Sutton Way SK9 7 G2
Swale Cl SK9 7 G5
Swan St SK9 8 D2
Swettenham Rd SK9 7 F2
Swinley Chase SK9 7 H6
Swiss Hill SK9 10 D2
Sycamore Cl SK9 6 D5
Sylvan Av SK9 8 B4

Tabley Rd SK9 7 F2
Talbot Rd SK9 10 D2
Tame Walk SK9 7 G5
Tarporley Walk SK9 7 G5
Tarvin Way SK9 7 F2
*Tatton Ct,
  Tatton Rd SK9 7 F2
Tatton Rd SK9 7 G2
Tempest Rd SK9 11 E3
The Avenue SK9 10 C2
The Circuit,
  Alderley Edge SK9 10 D1
The Circuit,
  Wilmslow SK9 8 A4
The Coppins SK9 8 A5
The Crescent SK10 11 H2
The Green SK9 7 G4
The Lawns SK9 8 A5
The Link SK9 7 F4
The Meade SK9 9 E1
The Race SK9 7 F5
The Ridings SK9 8 A5
The Stablings SK9 8 C4
Thirlmere Cl SK9 10 B2
Thistlewood Dr SK9 9 F2
Thoresway Rd SK9 8 B4
Thornfield Hey SK9 9 G1
Thorngrove Dr SK9 9 E3
Thorngrove Hill SK9 9 E4
Thorngrove Rd SK9 9 E3
Thornton Dr SK9 7 G4
Thurston Grn SK9 10 C3
*Tilston Walk,
  Lyngard SK9 7 G6
Timbersbrook Gro SK9 7 F5
Toft Way SK9 7 G3
*Torbrook Gro,
  Bosley Cl SK9 7 F5
Torkington Rd SK9 9 E3
Trafford Rd,
  Alderley Edge SK9 10 C2
Trafford Rd,
  Wilmslow SK9 6 D6
Tranmere Dr SK9 7 G5
Tudor Grn SK9 7 G6
Tudor Rd SK9 7 G6
Turnberry Dr SK9 9 F1
Twinnies Ct SK9 7 E6
Twinnies Rd SK9 6 D6
Tyler St SK9 10 C2

Ullswater Rd SK9 7 E3
Underwood Rd SK9 10 D2

Upcast La SK9 8 A
*Upton Way,
  Beeston Rd SK9 7 F

Vale Head SK9 7 G
Vale Rd SK9 8 E
Valley Dr SK9 7 E
Vardon Dr SK9 9 F
Victoria Rd SK9 8 C
Viewlands Dr SK9 7 F
Village Way SK9 7 F
*Wadebrook Gro,
  Malpas Cl SK9 7 G

Wadsworth Cl SK9 7 G
Wallingford Rd SK9 7 F
Wallworth Ter SK9 8 A
Walnut Cl SK9 9 G
Warburton Rd SK9 7 F
Wareham St SK9 9 G
Warren Hey SK9 9 G
Water La SK9 8 C
Waveney Dr SK9 7 F
Weaverham Way SK9 9 F
Welford Cl SK9 9 F
Welsh Row SK10 10 A
Welton Cl SK9 8 B
Welton Cl SK9 8 B
Welton Gro SK9 8 B
West Bank SK9 10 C
*West Holme Ct,
  Lynton La SK9 10 C
West St SK9 10 C
Westgate SK9 10 C
Westminster Dr SK9 8 C
Weston Rd SK9 8 B
Westward Rd SK9 8 B
Wheelock Cl SK9 7 F
Whitebarn Rd SK9 10 D
Whitehall Cl SK9 8 D
Wilcott Rd SK9 8 E
Wilkins La SK9 6 A
*Willaston Way,
  Sandiway Rd SK9 7 F
Willow Dr SK9 7 F
Wilmslow Pk North
  SK9 9 E
Wilmslow Pk South
  SK9 9 E
Wilmslow Rd,
  Alderley Edge SK9 10 C
Wilmslow Rd,
  Handforth SK9 7 F
Wilmslow Way SK9 9 E
Wilton Cres SK9 10 E
Winchester Cl SK9 8 A
Windermere Dr SK9 7 E
Windermere Rd SK9 7 E
Windsor Av SK9 8 E
Wingfield Av SK9 8 B
Wingfield Dr SK9 8 E
Woking Rd SK9 7 H
Wolverton Dr SK9 9 F
Wood Gdns SK9 10 D
Woodacres Ct SK9 8 E
*Woodcote Gro,
  Picton Dr SK9 7 G
Woodbrook Rd SK9 10 D
Woodcote Vw SK9 7 H
Woodlands Rd,
  Handforth SK9 7 G
Woodlands Rd,
  Wilmslow SK9 6 E
Woodleigh Ct SK9 10 C
Worms Hill SK9 6 C
Wycliffe Av SK9 8 C

Yew Tree Cl SK9 9 F
York Cres SK9 9 F